Mysteries
of the
New Testament

William Hoste

JOHN RITCHIE LTD
CHRISTIAN PUBLICATIONS

40 Beansburn, Kilmarnock, Scotland

ISBN-13: 978 1 909803 90 9

www.ritchiechristianmedia.co.uk

Typeset by John Ritchie Ltd., Kilmarnock
Printed by Bell & Bain Ltd., Glasgow

Mysteries of the New Testament.

Introduction.

THE subject of the "Mysteries" of the New Testament is one of the highest importance and interest. We touch here some of "the deep things of God." Here are "waters to swim in." We need, therefore, in a special manner, the Spirit's teaching. "The things of God knoweth no man, but the Spirit of God" (1 Cor. ii. 11). But we may surely with expectant faith claim the promise of our Lord—"He shall teach you all things,"—"He will guide you into all truth" (John xiv. 26 ; xvi. 13).

The word "mystery" does not occur in the Old Testament, but seems to correspond to the expression, "*dark sayings* of old" (Psa. lxviii. 2, see also Psa. xlix. 4 and Prov. i. 6), that is, sayings which have been kept dark, but which the Psalmist was inspired prophetically to reveal. I think this correspondence is shewn by the way this passage is quoted by the Lord in Matt. xiii. 35, "I will open my mouth in parables, I will utter *things which have been kept secret* from the foundation of the world."

The last phrase, "things which have been kept secret from (or even before) the foundation of the world" may serve well to explain the meaning of the word "mystery."

In modern speech, a mystery is something unintelligible and incompehensible, something baffling and even uncanny. But it does not bear this sense in the New Testament, any more than in classical Greek, from which it is derived. The word comes from the ancient mysteries—the Eleusinian, for instance—which were religious ceremonies or rites practised among the Greeks. They consisted of purifications, sacrifical offerings and processions, songs and dances. These rites were kept secret from all, except the initiated, but initiation was open to all who had the heart to seek it.

In the New Testament, the word has the same general sense : not something kept secret, but a secret revealed *for* all, but only *to* the initiated.

The word is derived from a verb *muein*—"to initiate," closely connected with another verb, "to close the lips, or eyes." The initiate was under obligation not to divulge the secrets learnt, and to close his eyes to all else.

This verb, "to initiate" only occurs once in the New Testament. "I have *learned* in whatsoever state I am, to be content " (Phil. iv. 11). The word is—"I have learned the secret." Paul had been initiated into the mysteries of His Father's love and wisdom. He was assured that all was well. The word "therewith " is in italics, and may well be omitted. He had learned to be content *in*—not with—his state of things. This is true Christian experience. The believer finds out what God is, as he passes through circumstances and learns contentment.

A "mystery," then, is not something that baffles solution, but a secret made known. There are mysteries which are "hard to be understood" (e.g., the mystery of I Cor. xv. 51), but this is incidental. That all living believers will be transformed when the Lord returns, is a truth revealed to faith, but how such an event is to take place is not explained. The fact that the word is usually linked with some such phrase as "made known" or "revealed," proves that the idea of a mystery is not of something which we may not know, but rather what has been made known by God Himself, for our instruction and edification.

But are not spiritual truths known only by the revelation of the Spirit of God ? And yet all are not mysteries. How shall we then distinguish between truths which are "mysteries" and those that are not ?

I believe that a "mystery" is a new and unexpected development of the purposes of God, in relation to some spiritual truth which may or may not have been revealed before—a surprise revelation, constituting something entirely new in the ways of God, though known to Him from the beginning. On the other hand, Creation, Redemption, Resurrection are all revealed truths, but they have not this feature of novel development. We may illustrate what is meant from a well known case in the Old Testament. That Joseph was in Egypt, could scarely be a "mystery" to his brothers.

They had sold him to merchants travelling thither, and he might well be there. But that Joseph had been raised by God to be the Governor of all the land of Egypt, and that for their deliverance and preservation, was something they could have no conception of whatever, until Joseph made himself known, and revealed to them the purpose of God·

The infant Moses is another case in point. That he would be providentially delivered from death was, I would judge, real to the faith of Amram and Jochebed, and for that Miriam was set to watch—" to wit what would be done to him " (Ex. ii. 4). She did not expect to see him devoured by evil beasts or drowned in the Nile, but delivered in some way or other by El-Shaddai, the All-sufficient God. But that the babe should be rescued by Pharaoh's daughter, confided to his own mother to nurse, and brought up in the palace of the very man who sought his life, was something worthy of God, a totally unexpected development, "exceeding abundant" above all that was asked or thought.

The same principle might be illustrated in the history of David, Esther, Daniel, and other saints of God. And so the apostle says, "We speak the wisdom of God in a mystery, the hidden wisdom, which God ordained before the world, ·unto our glory. . . But as it is written, Eye hath not seen, nor ear heard, neither hath entered into the heart of man, the things which God hath prepared for them that love Him. But God hath revealed them unto us by His Spirit, for the Spirit searcheth all things, yea, the deep things of God " (1 Cor. . 7-10).

Chapter I.

SEVEN GREAT MYSTERIES.

THE Divine mysteries are the secrets of God made known to His people "in due time." They come as the answer of God o e consistent failure of man, and to the apparent victories of Satan, to his confusion and to the praise of the saints, who with one voice exclaim, "How unsearchable are His judgments, and His ways past finding out !" (Rom. xi. 33).

The Satanic mysteries are the counterfeits of the Divine—the bitter Dead Sea fruit of the creature's rebellion come to full maturity. In them will be clearly proved, what was shewn at Calvary, the fearful and hopeless character of sin. They will be something novel, something startling, something more deliberately wicked than anything known before.

But when men have betrayed their trust and Satan done his worst, God brings out of His treasury something new, something unexpected, something better than was before, because containing a fuller revelation of Christ. For all is summed up in Him, "in whom are hid all the the treasures of wisdom and knowledge" (Col. ii. 3).

His atonement is the fulcrum on which the eternal counsels turn ; His glory the supreme object of all the purposes of God ; His Person the grand centre around which all else revolves. Of Him Jehovah says—" I have laid help upon One that is mighty ; I have exalted One chosen out of the people. I have found David My servant ; with My holy oil have I anointed Him " (Psa. lxxxviii. 19, 20). And faith rejoins, " Let Thy hand be upon the man of Thy right hand, upon the Son of Man whom Thou madest strong for Thyself "(Psa. lxxx. 17).

It is a vast relief to remember, in view of sad corporate as well as personal failure, that all God's purposes and our eternal blessings are in the pierced hands of Him, " who His own self bear our sins, in His own body on the tree " (1 Pet. ii. 24), whom now God has glorified at His own right hand in Heaven, and whose presence is assured to us through His Spirit " all the days, even to the end of the age " (Matt. xxviii. 20, R.·V.).

Early in the first Epistle to the Corinthians, the apostle disclaims the place of a denominational leader. It was indeed a signal honour put upon the apostles, that none of them founded sects. But later on in the Epistle, he indicates what he does claim to be. " Let a man so account of us as stewards of the Mysteries of God. But it is required in stewards, that a man be found faithful " (1 Cor. iv. 2).

Stewardship, involves responsibility. A steward must give account of his stewardship. In this matter, the apostle " knew nothing against (not by) himself." He who knew himself as " the chief of sinners," certainly lays no claim here to impeccability or infallibility. But he was not conscious of having betrayed his trust as " a steward of the mysteries. " He had not tampared with one of them, but as far as he knew, had declared " the whole counsel of God. " Let it be our ambition by grace, to do likewise.

Only three of the apostles, Matthew, John, and Paul, and two others, Mark and Luke, probably possessed of the prophetic gift, were commissioned to record the revelation of Divine Mysteries. But we need not suppose they alone had the understanding of them. We know at least concerning the great Mystery of Christ, that it was in general "revealed to His holy apostles and prophets by the Spirit " (Eph. iii. 5), though Paul was the chosen instrument for its official revelation to the churches. It had no doubt been widely preached long before the Epistle to the Ephesians was written (see Rom. xvi. 25, 26).

The Divine Mysteries are, as I judge, seven in number :—

1. The Mystery of the Kingdom (Matt. xiii. ; Mark iv., Luke viii.).
2. The Mystery of Israel's fall (Romans xi. 25).
3. The Mystery of the Rapture (1 Cor. xv. 51).
4. The Mystery of Christ (Rom. xvi.25 ; Eph.iii.-v.).
5. The Mystery of Godliness (1 Tim. iii. 16).
6. The Mystery of God (Rev. x. 7).
7. The Mystery of Universal Headship (Eph i 9 10).

Numbers four and five are called "Great Mysteries. " The Satanic mysteries are twain :—

1. The Mystery of Iniquity (1 Thess ii. 7).
2. The Mystery of Babylon (Rev. xvii. 5).

It may be well to add here, that the word "mystery" is sometimes used in a *secondary* sense in the New Testament, for a hidden spiritual truth, or for something figurative, as in I Cor. xiv. 2—"but in spirit he speaketh mysteries," which can hardly mean that whenever a man spake with tongues, he uttered the great Mysteries of God, but simply truths hidden till interpreted. In the same way, are the words, "the mystery of the seven stars," interpreted, as meaning the angels of the seven churches (Rev. i. 20). The word standing for a hidden figure needing explanation. "Angel" here, should be taken, I judge, literally, not figuratively, for how explain a figure by a figure ? The candlesticks mean literal churches, and "the angels" I submit, mean angelic beings. We know that such share in the government of the world (see Dan. x. 13, 20, 21), and are also "sent forth to minister for them who shall be heirs of salvation" (Heb. i. 14). The words we are considering would go to shew that this is not only to saints in their individual but in their corporate capacity. Knowing how natural "the worshipping of angels" is to the heart of man (see Col. ii 18 ; Rev. xix. 10 ; xxii. 8), the almost complete silence of Scripture as to the nature of their "deacon work" is explained. How serious to God must be the sin so prevalent in Christendom, of dedicating to angels, religious feast days and buildings !

Chapter II.

THE MYSTERY OF THE KINGDOM.

WE will consider this mystery first for the following reasons:—It stands first in order in the New Testatment. It was the only one revealed by the Lord when on earth, and it illustrates clearly the special character of a Mystery as already noted—a surprise development of a truth previously known in part.

"The Kingdom of God" was not a mystery. It was a frequent theme with Psalmists and prophets. The mention of Jehovah's "King" occurs again and again in the Old Testament as a title of the Messiah. As such, He was the "Hope of Israel," not only in His sufferings, but in the glory that should follow. Psalm ii. speaks of His appointment: "Yet have I set My King upon My holy hill of Zion" (ver. 6). Psalm xxiv. answers the question, "Who is the King of glory ? The Lord strong and mighty, the Lord mighty in battle." In Psa. lxxii. we have an attractive and comprehensive picture of the extent and and characteristics of the coming Kingdom. Isaiah ix. unfolds some of the glories of the King's Name : "Wonderful, Counsellor, the Mighty God, the Everlasting Father, the Prince of Peace." Chap. xi. describes the effects of His rule—righteousness, peace, universal knowledge of .

God, and blessing to Israel. Daniel dwells on its all-embracing and eternal character, "a Kingdom which shall never be destroyed and . . shall be given to the people of the saints of the Most High, whose Kingdom is an everlasting Kingdom, and all dominions shall serve and obey Him"(chap. ii. 44).

These are only a few out of numberless passages where the Kingdom is foretold in the Old Testament. Later on, it was the Kingdom which John the Baptist and the Lord Himself heralded. And when Christ taught His disciples to pray "Thy Kingdom come," it was no mere spiritual blessing they were to ask for, but that the literal Kingdom of God should be set up on the earth. This idea of the Kingdom, therefore, was perfectly well understood. But the Kingdom in *Mystery* was a new revelation, not once breathed before its mention in Matthew xiii. This chapter (see also Mark iv. and Luke viii.) marked a new departure in our Lord's testimony. He now begins to speak in parables of the Mystery or Mysteries of the Kingdom,* and why? Because "the Kingdom" in the hitherto known sense was rejected. Each of these three chapters in the Synoptic Gospels is immediately preceded by a clear indication of this rejection. What else did the imprisonment of John mean (Luke vii.)? What else the blasphemous imputation that the

* In Matt. xiii. the Lord gives seven parables of the Kingdom. In Mark iv. we have the first and third—the sower and the mustard tree, and an eighth, not found in Matthew, the parable of the growing seed (v. 26-29), all three, indeed, "seed" parables. In Luke viii. we find the first, and in chap. xiii. the third and fourth.

very mighy works which proved that the King was in their midst, were done in league with Beelzebub? (Matt. xii.), The Kingdom had "come unto them," but they had wilfully rejected it, in the person of their leaders. This was the first act in the rejection of the King. What, then, must happen? Clearly the literal Kingdom could not be then set up, for how could it exist in the absence of the rejected King? That it was to be set up in a new, undreamed of character, was a fresh revelation by Christ to His own. This is the Kingdom in Mystery. Its special characteristics are illustrated in the seven parables of Matthew xiii.

The Seven Parables of The Kingdom.

These parables do not present a consecutive panorama of the Kingdom in Mystery, but are separate tableaux of it in its moral aspects as seen by God ; this one covering the whole period ; that one shewing a special development, others again running on contemporaneously. The special characteristics of the Kingdom in Mystery are :—

1. *It is the Realm of a Rejected King.*—It extends over the period of Christ's rejection, and ends with His return to establish the earthly kingdom ; as the words twice repeated in verses 48 and 49 shew— "So shall it be in the end of the world" (or age). The Church is not seen *as such* in this chapter. The Kingdom begins before and extends beyond the Church period. Believers in this dispensation are seen here as "children of the Kingdom." But though the Lord is absent in body, He is present by His Spirit. To bow to His authority even now

is incumbent on all, for "He is Lord of all" (Acts x. 36).

2. *It is Hidden from the eyes of men.*—For this the Lord speaks here in parables. "The kingdom of God is not meat and drink (does not consist of outward, tangible rites), but righteousness, peace, and joy in the Holy Ghost" (Rom. xiv. 17)—fruits of His Lordship obeyed in the heart. "The Kingdom of God cometh not with observation," it is within (Luke xvii. 20). The figures used, speak of its hidden character. Seed germinating, leaven permeating, treasure hid in a field, a drag-net operating unseen beneath the waves.

3. *In it, the Good appears to Fail.*—The Sower sows the Divine Word, but the ground is hard and unprepared, so that much good seed is lost. In the second parable, the influence of that good seed— the children of the Kingdom—is met by the presence of the tares—Satan's counterfeit witnesses.

4. *In it, the False seems to Prevail.*—Multitudes with only a name to live, take their place in the Kingdom. They name the Name of Christ, but do not depart from iniquity. The mustard seed, instead of remaining a humble annual, becomes an abormal perennial—a great growth, rivalling Nebuchadnezzar's tree (Dan. iv.). The big attracts. Hence the success of the bad in the third parable. In the fourth, the success of the bad seems guaranteed, because it is in its very nature to spread, except where, through grace, sight enables the evil to be put away. The three measures of fine flour, representing the pure, unsullied doctrine of Christ, are permeated with that which has but one mean-

ing in the Scriptures—evil, doctrinal, moral, political.

5. *"God's Purposes are ripening fast."*—This is taught in the parables of the Treasure and the Pearl, and in the eighth parable of Mark iv, the seed which "springs up, he knoweth not how, " in the power of resurrection life. At least, in the first two, we see the Lord at work purchasing and manifesting His own. The Treasure, be it noted, is not a bag of specie or precious stones, detachable from the field, but something bound up with the field, like a mine of precious metal. Why else must the field be bought ? The Treasure thus, I believe, represents the elect of Israel. Jehovah's " special treasure" (Mal. iii. 17, mar.), inseparably connected with the earth, by the promises made unto the fathers. The spot where the treasure is found is Palestine, but its possession necessitates the purchase of the whole earth, The Pearl cannot properly speaking be the Church as such, though it includes it, for how could the disciples understand that which was not yet revealed ? That they were expected to understand the Lord's words, and did in fact do so, is evidenced by our Lord's question and their answer (see Matt. xiii. 51). The Pearl is, I believe, the whole glorious aggregate of the children of the Kingdom. The purchase, both of the Treasure and the Pearl, entailed the sacrifice of all else. "Ye know the grace of our Lord Jesus Christ, that though He was rich, yet for your sakes He became poor, that ye through His poverty might become rich. " And the same "precious blood" that redeemed our souls, has purchased this planet.

B

He is now the lawful Owner of the field by purchase, as well as creation, so that none but He can break the seven seals of the title-deeds of the "inheritance" (Rev. v.).

6. *In it, His Spirit works on all.*—The mighty force of the drag-net in the last parable, symbolises this divine energy of His working on the hearts and consciences of men. God has never left Himself without a witness, much less will He do so in the last solemn days of the Spirit's testimony, when the time for such testimony is rapidly vanishing away.

7. *It will need Purging.*—All who come under the Spirit's sway and yield outward obedience to His influences, do not eventually prove to be true "children of the Kingdom." Bad and good are gathered in, and the testing day alone will reveal the character of each. We do not read that Christ will purge His Church at His return. He is doing so now. Then He will "present it to Himself a glorious Church, not having spot or wrinkle or any such thing,." But when He comes again as the Son of Man He will purge His Kingdom. "He will send forth His angels and gather out of His Kingdom all things that offend, and they which work iniquity" (things and men, stumbling blocks, and lawless persons). And " THEN shall the righteous shine forth as the sun, in* the "Kingdom of their Father" (v. 43). Then will be revealed also to the world the Mystery of the Kingdom—that through seeming defeat, the Lord was reigning. Yes, "the Lord·

*For a fuller treatment of this subject, see " The Kingdom of God: Its Subjects and Scope." By the present writer. Just issued. price 3d. May be had from J. Ritchie, Kilmarnock.

reigneth " even in these dark and difficult times. Nor has He resigned either rod or sceptre into His people's hands. This surely ought to give confidence and comfort to those who are called to bear witness for His Name in these last days, of departure from the truth.

Chapter III.

THE MYSTERY OF
THE HEAVENLY REMNANT.

Romans xi. 1-25.

THIS Mystery is the first referred to in the Epistles, and is connected with God's present dealings with Israel. In this age they are cut off, as branches from their own olive tree—the similitude used in this chapter to describe their place of national privilege. The Gentile nations, though branches of a wild olive tree, are now grafted contrary to nature into the place of privilege. But "God hath not *cast away* His people which He foreknew." They will be grafted in again, and even now there are some branches left, for "Even at this present time, there is a remnant according to the election of grace" (ver. 5). What then is the Mystery? It is not that blindness should happen to Israel. That was clearly foretold by Moses, if they disobeyed God, "The Lord shal smite thee with . . blindness" (Deut. xxviii. 28 and by Isaiah and David, as quoted here (Rom. xi. 8, 9). But that this blindness should be partial, is now for the first time made known to us. "I would not, brethren, that ye should be ignorant of this Mystery, that blindness in *part* is happened to Israel, until the fulness of the Gentiles be come in "

(Rom. xi. 25). This Mystery then, is connected with the remnant of Israel in this dispensation, and especially with the peculiar character of that remnant. It is no new thing for God to reserve to Himself a remnant out of Israel. He did so, as we shall see, after the Babylonian captivity. He will do so in the last apostate days of Antichrist. But it is important to notice that in both these cases, the remnant is the representative of the nation in connection with earthly blessing and their national hope. The remnant we are now considering is to distinguished *from Israel* nationally and religiously, and enters into blessing of quite another order.* It is a Heavenly Remnant. This was something unheard of in Old Teatatment times, and is one more unexpected and surprising development in the ways of God.

The Epistle to the Romans falls naturally into three divisions—(1) Doctrinal, chaps. i.-viii. ; (2) Dispensational, chaps. ix.-xi.; (3) Practical, chaps. xii.-xvi. It is with the central division we have to do here. The word "Dispensation" is from a Greek noun, which is sometimes translated "steward-ship" (Luke xvi. 2, 3, 4). and means a principle of God's dealing with His creatures. These dispensations have been varied. From the Fall to the Flood, man was left without Law and Govern-

---

* We do not expect to find in Romans a full exposition of the Mystery of the Church, but it is clear that there could be no remnant of Israel recognized as an earthly remnant in the present Church period. An understanding of this would have saved people from the mistake of interpreting Matthew xxiv. in terms of the Church, when Israel is clearly in view as such, or of making the Church go through "the time of Jacob's trouble," which is only another name for " The Great Tribulation."

ment, to the light of conscience. From the Flood to the call of the Chosen Nation, He was placed under Government. Then followed God's dealings with Israel under Government and Law, with room for grace to act in virtue of the sacrifices. Now is the dispensation of Grace, in which is being unfolded the mystery of the Heavenly Remnant we are now considering. But what is a remnant? It is that which God reserves to Himself in view of general failure. "What saith the answer of God to Elias? "I have reserved to Myself seven thousand men, who have not bowed the knee to the image of Baal" (ver. 4). This was the remnant of Israel in Ahab's wicked days, and there always has been such a remnant according to the "election of grace." We may note four remnants in the history of the Chosen Race. (1) Spiritual or Figurative (2) Historical, (3) Prophetic, (4) Heavenly.

Chap. ix. of our Epistle, presents us the first— "a remnant according to the election of grace." The passage from the eighth to the ninth of Romans, is as from July sun to Autumn chill. The apostle puts off the garment of praise for a spirit of heaviness, as he turns from the contemplation of the glories of Christ, to view the sad condition of "his kinsmen according to the flesh." He yearns over them with the affections of Christ. He would wish to be anathema* for them. Had ever a people such privileges? Had not the Saviour sprung from them, "Christ who is over

---

* Christ is never said to be "Anathema." The word in Gal. iii. 13, "being made a curse for us," is a distinct word (Katara), which also occurs in Heb. vi. 8 and James iii. 10. "Anathema" is the word in 1 Cor. xii. 3, and Gal. i. 8-9.

all, God blessed for ever ? " And yet they were not saved, for instead of receiving " Him, who is the end of the law for righteouness to every one that beliveth, " they were seeking by the works of he law " to establish their own righteouness." This did not show that God's promise had failed. He had given no pledge that all Israelites should be saved ; " for they are not all Israel which are of Israel." A man might be of the seed of Abraham, and not be a child of promise ; a son of Isaac, and yet despise his birthright.

It will repay us to study carefully in their Old Testatment settings, the quotations throughout this chapter. The two quotations regarding Jacob and Esau are separated by the whole range of Old Testament Scripture. The first, " The elder shall serve the younger, " was spoken before their birth, and was the sovereign decree of God, involving nothing but good to either brother ; the other, " Jacob have I loved and Esau have I hated," was uttered through Malachi, fifteen centuries later, and marks the effect of the responsible choice of Esau and his race, in their persistent enmity to the people of God. None but the rebellious or the sentimentalist can dispute God's right to have mercy on whom He will have mercy, and to harden those who persist, like Pharaoh, in resisting His will.* These latter will become the " vessels of

* Rom. ix. 15-18 should be studied in the light of the Old Testament history. It will be seen, that had mercy depended on man's will, and on man's running after God, none would have received it. Pharaoh's life was prolonged (Exodus ix. 13-16, R.V.), when he might have been righteously cut off, that he might serve as an object lesson of God's wrath and power.

wrath fitted for destruction ;" and the former " vessels of mercy prepared" by God "unto glory." In Israel, there were always two circles—an outer one of national privilege entered by birth and circumcision, and an inner one of grace, entered by repentance and faith in God. These latter, always proved the spiritual remnant, corresponding to the 7000 in Elijah's day.

Later on, there was another remnant of a different character, the Historic Remnant that returned from Babylon. God had promised by Jeremiah, that after 70 years of captivity accomplished, He would cause His people to return to Jerusalem. When the moment struck, Cyrus was stirred up to make a decree, that all who wished might return and build. It was an offer to all, but most preferred the quiet life in Babylon. About 42,000 responded, "whose spirit God had raised." They were spoken of by Ezra as a "remnant." "And now for a little space, grace hath been shewed from the Lord our God to leave us a remnant to escape " (chap. ix. 8). And also by Nehemiah (chap. i. 3). These met with great opposition, but became once more the representatives of the nation, in their land. Later, in the days of Malachi, they had greviously declined, but even then there was little living remnant, "who feared the Lord and thought upon His Name." These were the progenitors of the Simeons, the Annas, and the rest who "looked for redemption in Israel," and were ready to receive the Lord. In the last days, there will be another Remnant— referred to frequently in the prophets—which we may call the Prophetic Remnant. Isaiah speaks of them. " Except the Lord of hosts had left unto us a very small remnant, we should have been as Sodom " (chap. i. 9). " The remnant shall return, even the remnant of Jacob, unto the mighty God, though Thy people Israel be as the sand of the sea, yet a remnant (and a remnant only) shall return " (x. 22). These two verses are quoted in Rom. ix. as teaching generally, that God will have a spiritual seed from Israel in these days. But this is far from exhausting their meaning : in fact, it is an application rather than a fulfilment. Joel speaks undoubtedly of this latter day remnant. " In Mount Zion and in Jerusalem shall be deliverance, as the Lord hath said, and in the remnant whom the Lord shall call " (chap. ii. 32). This remnant will play an important role in the closing days. When the " Prince that shall come," aided and abetted by Israel's false king, the Antichrist, breaks his covenant with Israel in the midst of "the week," and causes the sacrifice and the oblation of Jehovah to cease (Dan. ix. 27), the nation as a whole will apostatise. But the remnant will remain faithful, and will be sustained by God amid terrible persecution, called in Jeremiah "the time of Jacob's trouble " (chap. xxx. 7). Many of the Psalms, such as the 94th, 130th, 140th, describe the sufferings of these witnesses. Those who are spared till the return of the Messiah, will be saved—according to Rom. xi 26, " And so all Israel shall be saved," and will form the nucleus of the restored nation. They are, I believe, those whom the Lord refers to as "My brethren " at the judgment of the nations (Matt. xxv. 40). It remains for us now to consider briefly the calling and character of the Heavenly Remnant. They are those who through the preaching of the Gospel in this dispensation, are brought to acknowledge Jesus as Lord and Saviour. They are sometimes called to-day, " Hebrew-Christians," but it is really a misnomer. They are Christians, members of that body in which there is "neither Jew nor Greek." Israel has rejected Christ, and He who might have been their Corner-stone has become their stumbling stone. They were judged and scattered in 70 A.D., and through their fall, salvation is come unto the Gentiles for to provoke them to jealousy. Not, of course, that all Gentiles are saved, but they are now in the olive tree. Instead of being in a less favoured position than Israel, it is they who are the favoured ones, and the Gospel is sounded to them in every place. Thus the fall of Israel brings opportunity to the Gentiles, and they draw from the root and fatness of the olive tree. All of them who believe on Jesus Christ are brought into the Church, and with them all who believe from Israel. If, then, the " fall " of Israel is " the riches of the Gentiles, how much more (according to the blessed logic of Divine grace) their fulness ?" If God blessed the Gentiles because of of Israel's fall, He will not take away that blessing when Israel is restored. Through restored Israel will come a wider blessing than ever was known before. Now the Lord is gathering out a people, and the results seem sparse, but when Israel are grafted back into their own olive tree and become God's missionaries to every land, in the power of the great outpouring of the Spirit yet to come (see

Joel ii. 28, 29), untold numbers will be gathered in,
" a great multitude that no man can number." The
Heavenly Remnant we are now considering is
composed of Israelites who believe the Gospel, and
are baptised into one body in one Spirit, with all
of every nation who receive Christ. Such lose
their national standing and hopes, but enter into
higher privileges and blessings, as members of
Christ and temples of the Holy Ghost. This state
of things will go on "until the fulness of the
Gentiles is come in," tha is until the last Gentile
destined to be a member of the church, is saved.
Then the church will be caught up, the Gentile
branches who have abused their privileges, broken
off, and God will resume His relations with the
nation of Israel. It was a very real test for a Jew
who had believed in Christ to find himself cut off
from his glorious historic past, shorn of his national hopes of the coming kingdom, and deprived of
his traditional priesthood and religion, every part
of which had been divinely ordained. It was for
such, the Epistle to the Hebrews was written. In
it, they might learn that all has been more than
made up to them in Christ, who is the consummation
of the prophetic testimony, the embodiment of the
kingdom hope, and the substance of all the religious
shadows of the past.

Chapter IV.

THE MYSTERY OF
THE GREAT TRANSFORMATION.

"BEHOLD, I shew you a mystery ; we shall not all sleep, but we shall all be changed" (I Cor. xv. 51.). The mysteries of God are undreamt of dispays of His "manifold wisdom" and boundless reserves of grace and power ; foretastes of those eternal revelations of Himself which will for ever be the joy of the redeemed. "This is life eternal, that they might know Thee the only true God, and Jesus Christ, whom Thou hast sent" (John xvii. 3). The knowledge of God in Christ not only communicates eternal life, but characterises it and that for ever. In the case before us, the revelation is made in full view of man's failure, The rejection of the Spirit's testimony to a crucified and glorified Saviour, must lead at length to the Apocalyptic judgments. Must the Church then pass through them ? Had we only the Old Testament, it would appear inevitable. But would not a king, before attacking a rebellious city, seek first, if possible, to take out of it any faithful subjects within, as Saul called forth the Kenites before attacking Amalek ? The "mystery" we are about to consider, is a way of escape for the Church, from

" the hour of temptation that will come upon the whole world," or, in other words, from the Great Tribulation.   The fifteenth of First Corinthians and the fourth of First Thessalonians, are the the passages which present us this deliverance in most detail, though it is referred to in many others. These two Scriptures are parallel, and should be carefully compared, for they emphasise different phases of the same truth. In the Thessalonian Epistle, much is said of the actual coming of Christ, and of the meeting of the saints with Him.   " The Lord Himself shall descend from heaven . . we shall be caught up together . . to meet the Lord in the air."   In the Corinthian passage, neither of these events is mentioned specifically, but much attention is drawn to the processes which will take place in the sleeping and living saints— resurrection and transformation—at the moment of the coming.   In the former church, the question seems to have been raised—"What will become of the sleeping saints when the Lord returns ?   Will they have no share in that event ?"   While in the fifteenth of First Corinthians the problem is—"If flesh and blood cannot inherit the Kingdom of God," what will become of the living saints ? Must they be excluded ?"   The answer to the last difficulty forms the thesis of the passage before us. It may be called the " Mystery of the Great Transformation," and as such regarded from two points

* We may remind ourselves in passing, that the Thessalonian Epistle was written from Corinth according to the best authorities, during the apostle's stay referred to in Acts xviii., and that addressed to the Corinthians, during his stay in Ephesus, as narrated in Acts xix.

of view: (1) the *Power* that will produce the effect —the Coming of the Lord, and (2) the *Character* of the effect produced—Resurrection and Metamor- phosis.

The coming of the Son of Man to judge was no mystery. The Old Testament prophecies are full of it (see Psa. l., xcvi., xcvii. ; Isa. lviii. ; Joel ii.- iii. ; Zech. xii., xiv., etc.), but always in connection with antecedent tribulation. "When the Son of Man cometh, shall He find faith on the earth ?" (Luke xviii. 8). No, but a world desolated by judg- ment, the faithful remnant of Israel under the heel of the oppressor, and man in open apostacy and rebellion against God—a condition of things closely analogous with that existing in Egypt before the Exodus of Israel. God will then be dealing once more in judgment with a greater than Pharaoh, to deliver the same people from a worse oppression than that of Egypt. And they, too, will suffer as before from these same judgments. The coming of the Son of Man will be the supreme crisis in the long period called "the day of the Lord," inter- vening at the moment when Jacob's trouble will have reached its utmost intensity. "I beheld, and the same horn made war with the saints, and prevailed against them, until the Ancient of Days came " (Dan. vii. 22, 25 ; see also Zech. xiv. 2-4). This corresponds with the coming in vengeance spoken of in 2 Thess. i. 7, 8, and the appearing of the "Faithful and True" in Rev. xix. 11. This is the same phase that we have in the great prophetic discourses of our Lord in the Synoptic Gospels. The words in Matt. xxiv., "One shall be taken and

another left," are often interpreted as referring to
the "catching up" of the saints as in 1 Thess. iv·
17, but I believe this to be erroneous. Surely the
"taking "* in Matt. xxiv. 40, 41, corresponds with
what has just gone in verse 29, "the flood came and
took them (*i.e.*, the wicked) all away." Whereas in
1 Thess. iv. 17, the righteous will be taken away
while the wicked are left for judgment. To sum
up : the coming of the Son of Man was already well
known, but that there should be a previous stage in
His coming, to take away the saints "from the evil
to come," was a "Mystery" unheard of by the
prophets of old. Was not this in our Lord's mind
(though He explains not the how and the wherefore), when to His sorrowing disciples He speaks
of His speedy return, not now as "the Son of Man,"
but in the first person—"I will come again and
receive you unto Myself, that where I am, there ye
may be also ?" Here, there is no word of "heavenly
signs," or "flaming fire," nor of "vengeance," or
"mighty angels," but the calm, clear atmosphere
of the joyful meeting, far above all the fogs and
din of this dark scene, If the question be asked,
whether or not the Old Testament will end before
the New, it will suffice to read the closing chapter
of each, and ask whether or not the "Morning
Star" rises before the "Sun." Then, again, we may
consider the effect to be produced. The resurrection

* It is true, that the words in the original for " taking away,'
and ' take " are not the same. The context alone can determine
the purport of the " taking " in verses 40 and 41, and also of the
" leaving "—which may well have the meaning " let go " (Mark
xi. 6). or " let alone " (Mark xiv. 6 ; Luke xiii. 8).

of the dead was not a mystery. The Sadducees, had they known the Scriptures, should have believed this much, and by the Scriptures, too, the religious world of our day might have been preserved from the idea which is so prevalent of a "general resurrection." The expression, "the resurrection of life," and the "resurrection of judgment," though occurring in the same verse (John v. 29), are sufficiently distinct to save from this error.

At least "a thousand years" must elapse between the two resurrections (see Rev. xx. 5). We may notice first, that the resurrection spoken of in 1 Cor. xv. is *Selective*. The resurrection of the body is the great truth of the whole chapter. Properly speaking, resurrection always pertains to the body. It is quite certain that the wicked will have a resurrection body—"to every seed his own body"—prepared of God, according to His determinate purpose. But though the resurrection of the wicked may be incidentally included in such an expression as "*the* resurrection of the dead*" (v. 13), the subject of the chapter practically all through, is the resurrection of sleeping saints. How could verses 42-49 refer to the ungodly ? Their resurrection body could not be described as " glorious " or "heavenly." There is "a first resurrection," and there is a final resurrection. Only "the just" will share in the first. "Blessed and holy is he that hath part in the first resurrection" (Rev. xx. 6). Only the wicked will share in the last. "They were judged by every man according to their works." They had not therefore been justified by faith, but were still in their sins.

There is no thought in Scripture of a "general judgment" of saints and sinners before the great white throne. If saints are there at all (as 1 Cor. vi. 2, 3, would seem to indicate), they will be as assessors on the throne, not as prisoners before it. Those, then, who are said in 1 Cor. xv. 54, to "put on incorruption," are the sleeping saints, the rest* of the dead remain in their graves till the fina resurrection of "the dead, small and great." So much for the saints who have died. Now for the living. That there will be godly persons alive on the earth when the Son of Man returns, is abundantly clear from such passages as Zech. xii. 10. "They shall look on Me whom they have pierced," is spoken of the spared remnant of Israel. But that there should be a company of persons alive when the Lord returns, and instantly changed and fitted by "putting on immortality" to stand before Him and to enter His heavenly kingdom, was a truth hitherto unheard of. It is to this, therefore, that the words of the apostle—"We shall not all sleep, but we shall all be changed"—more directly apply. It is clear that none but believers will have part in this wonderful transformation scene. The hope of Israel is, to be carried through the great tribulation, as Noah was through the flood, and like him to enter on possession of a renovated earth. The hope of the Church is, to be taken away before the judgments fall, as Enoch was, by translation from earth to heaven. The exhortation in Luke xxi. 36,

* Those raised in Rev. xx. 4, are expressly said to have sealed their testimony with their blood in the great tribulation, at the hands of the Beast.

is not addressed to Christians, that they should pray to be caught away when Christ comes, inasmuch as this is part of their heritage as believers, but to pious Israelites that they may be preserved *through* the coming troubles, and be alive on the earth, when the Son of Man shall return in His glory. The truth of this coming, could not but be associated in the minds of Israel with the thought of tribulation. The dread valley lay deep and dark between, and so it would be for the Church, but for the revelation of the rapture of the saints. And THIS is the hope of the Church, and the more we are walking with God in separation from the world, and suffering practically with and for Christ, this hope will become bright and sustaining.

One of the world's great texts is, "It is appointed unto *all men* to die," but the Scriptures say, "It is appointed unto *men* once to die, and after this the judgment" (Heb ix. 27). "*We shall not all sleep, but we shall all be changed.*" This is the "sleep" of death, from which the word "cemetery" is derived. None but true believers, strickly speaking, should be buried in a cemetery—*i.e.*, a sleeping place—for *they* only " fall asleep." All others DIE. Now the "body is dead (exposed to death or mortality) because of sin, but the spirit is life, because of righteousness " (Rom. viii. 10). Then shall be fulfilled that quickening of which the apostle straightway speaks in ver. 11—"He that raised up Christ from the dead, shall also quicken your mortal bodies by His Spirit which dwelleth in you." God is the Source of this great change, His Spirit the Power, and the Lord Jesus at His coming, the Agent.

" When He shall appear we shall be like Him for we shall see Him as He is " (John iii. 2). It is an unsound exegesis which interprets this verse of some *present* healing or strengthening of the body for service. The change referred to must be something commensurate with the mighty work of the resurrection of Christ—the great manifestation to the Church of the " exceeding greatness if His power "—just as the works of creation are to the heathen, and the deliverance from Egypt to Israel. What else then could be an adequate fulfilment of this promise, but that instantaneous and simultaneous transformation of myriads of living saints in a moment of time referred to here, the " changing of the body of their humiliation into the likeness of His glorious body." The expression, "your mortal bodies," in Rom. viii. 11, points to the fact, that the apostle was not contemplating the resurrection of these saints in view of their death, but of their transformation, as in 2 Cor, v. 4, "that mortality might be swallowed up of life." This will only apply to believers, for they only are waiting for the " adoption, to wit the redemption of the body." So that we may call this *selective* as regards the world in general.

But it will be *Universal* as regards believers. I do not think we have Scripture for limiting the resurrection in I Cor. xv, and I Thess. 14 to believers of this dispensation alone. Of course, if the phrase, " those who sleep in Jesus " in I Thess. iv., were accurate, we must do so. But the Greek is confessedly " through " (see R. V. margin), not " in." Is not the thought here rather, how the sleeping ones will be restored to those they love, "by" or "through Jesus," rather than how they were taken away from them. The word "sleep" is sufficient to limit the application to those who have died in the faith. As regards the "changed" ones, we may safely affirm that they are all Christians, for there is no other kind of believer on the earth to-day. There is at any rate no authority for excluding any saint of this dispensation, from either the resurrection or the change. The hope of the Lord's appearing is one of the seven privileges in which all believers now share. "There is one body and one Spirit, even as ye are called *in one hope* of your calling" (Eph. iv. 5). There ought not indeed to be room for doubt on this point in the mind of any believer subject to the Word of God, for the affirmation could not be plainer. "We shall ALL be changed." "The DEAD (not some of them) shall be raised incorruptible." No hint is given, that some of the saints will be excluded.

Again, the change will be *Instantaneous.* "In a moment, in the twinkling of an eye"—both of which words are only used in the New Testament in this place, serving thus to mark the absolutely unique character of the event.

The Lord's coming for His own will take place *at a Special Signal.* "At the last trump." To the world, this expression speaks of the great final judgment "at the end of the world," as it is termed. But we read of no trumpet blast at the Great White Throne. Nor can there be any reference here to the Seven Apocalyptic Trumpets. "The seventh," which sounds (see Rev. xi. 15), is not called "the last trumpet," nor is it accompanied by the miraculous transformation of the living saints, but rather by judgment and wrath against the nations. And in any case, it will not sound until much later than the events of our chapter. May we not find help in Num. x. in the use of both silver trumpets for the convocation of the assembly ? " When they (the priests) shall blow with them, ALL the assembly shall assemble themselves to thee ?" In the summoning of this solemn assembly of the heavenly people, it may be, that the first trump will wake the dead and the last will change the living. Certainly the words, "at the last trump," seem to belong to what has just gone before, the change of the living. And may not the other phrase, " for the trumpet shall sound," describe the first blast which summons the sleepers from their graves. In Thessalonians we simply read, " The Lord Himself shall descend from heaven with a shout, with the voice of the Archangel, and with the trump of God," but there is no diffierentiation as to first or last blast.

The change will be a *Radical* one. The bodies of the sleeping saints are viewed here in their corruption. They will put on what is essential to them—incorruptibility. But this is not said of the living. In their case the body is not said to be " corruptible " but " mortal," and they will therefore " put on immortality." In either case, the change will be essential, and will mean for both dead and living, the possession of a glorified body, "like unto His glorious body " (Phil. iii. 21), spiritual, powerful, heavenly. The soul is not in question here, but "this mortal," that is the body. The soul is never once said to be "mortal" in the whole range of Scripture, and could not properly be said to put on what it has never lost. Death is not a ceasing to exist, any more than life means merely "to exist." The eternal existence of man is a fundamental truth of God's Word, ever since "God breathed into man's nostrils the breath of life (a thing He never did to the beasts of the fields), and man became a living soul." This truth is bound up with man's responsibility and God's sovereign right to judge. The Christian receives pardon, justification, adoption, eternal life, union with Christ, the Holy Spirit, and many other blessings. Why is he never said to receive the gift of eternal existence ? Because he has it already, by the fact of his creation. The phrase, "Conditional Immortality," is a figment of man's brain, without any corresponding reality in God's Word. But is it not said in 1 Tim. vi. 16, that "God *only* hath immortality ?" Yes, but this is not the same as saying "God only is immortal," as the passage before us proves. For here are persons spoken of as "putting on immortality." Without controversy, the angels are immortal. Whoever heard of an angel receiving immortality as a special gift ? They are created so. God only has it in the essential sense in Himself, and He alone bestows it. The word "immortality" (*athanasia*) only occurs in 1 Tim. vi. 16, and in our passage in 1 Cor. xv. In other places it ought to be "incorruptibility," as the Greek (*aptharsia*) shows.

The change will also be an *Abiding One.* That

this should be called in question may seem incredible, yet men are being found to teach that certain " faithful " Christians, who have shared in this great resurrection scene, will later on, as a punishment for their sins, "temporarily return to corruption." Such a statement is as senseless as it is subversive. To say that that which has "put on incorruption " will be corrupted, is a contradiction in terms. Were it possible, by what power, we may ask, would the unhappy Christian be transformed again ? No, let us be sure that " whatsoever God doeth it shall be for ever, nothing can be put to it, neither can anything be taken from it, and God doeth it, that men may fear before Him" (Eccl. iii. 14).

This great transformation will be *a Seal of Victory*. " Then shall be brought to pass the saying which is written, Death is swallowed up in victory." The death of every Christian is a victory, for of each it can be said, " he is not dead, but sleepeth," for the sting of death pierced the heart of Christ, and there is none left for the believer. But the scene we are now considering is a victory manifest, and now on a grander scale than ever before, for He who died rose again, triumphant over death and the grave. Millions will then be delivered from the grave. Myriads will escape from dying. It is to be noted that this is not the *fulfilment* of the Old Testament prophecy (Isa. xxv. 8). It does not say " fulfilled " here, but only " brought to pass," an important difference, as may be noted in other places (e.g., Acts ii. 16). "This is that which hath been spoken." The fulfilment will come later in Israel's history, as will also the fulfilment of the quotation before us (taken from Isa. xxv. 8), when "the first resurrection" will stand complete, in the resurrection of the martyred witnesses of the last days.

The hope of this change is the *Basis of Present Endeavour*. "Wherefore, my beloved brethren, be ye steadfast, unmoveable, always abounding in the work of the Lord ; forasmuch as ye know that your labour is not in vain in the Lord." "The night cometh when no man can work."

Chapter V.

THE MYSTERY OF GODLINESS.

OF the mysteries revealed in the Word of God, two are specially designated as "great" by the Holy Spirit—the Mystery of Christ, and the Church," and the "Mystery of Godliness," in the passage before us. And confessedly great they are, both being closely linked with Him who is "the Great God and our Saviour Jesus Christ."

"The Mystery of Godliness" is often expounded as though it were equivalent to the "mystery of God," but "godliness" is not an attribute of God, but an attitude of man toward God. The word occurs in eight other places in the Epistle, and always as describing a certain character of life and conduct : "Exercise thyself rather unto godliness," "Godliness is profitable unto all things," "Shew godliness at home." Surely here, in the remaining occurrence, the word must bear the meaning. The godly man is the Godfearing man, who takes God into account, and lives subject to Him. The "Mystery of godliness" must reveal a life of perfect submission to God, in contrast with "the mystery of lawlessness," to be manifested later in the "son of perdition," who will "exalt himself above all that is called God" (2 Thess. ii. 4).

The apostle has been laying down from the beginning of chap. ii., the godly ordering of the assembly in their gatherings for prayer, Scriptural relations of the sexes, oversight and ministry, in order that Timothy—and through him others— might know how to behave "in the house of God, which is the church of the living God." Any other order would be disorder ; any other behaviour, misbehaviour. To emphaise this, he adds that the church is "the pillar and ground of the truth "; not the truth itself, nor the originator of it, but responsible to uphold it. How this responsibility is increaed by the greatness of the truth to be upheld! "Without controversy, great is the Mystery of godliness *God was manifest in the flesh."

Now, godliness in itself was not a "mystery." It had characterised the lives of the saints of God from Abel onwards. The word, "Khaseed," is often found in the law and the prophets, and translated "godly, or holy one." "Let thy Urim . . be with

* It would not be in place here to argue this much disputed reading, which a prince of scholars—Dr. Scrivener—has called the "crux of the cities." Whether the passage ought to read as above, or simply " Who was manifest in the flesh," does not so profoundly effect the sense as might at first appear. The truth embodied in "God" is implied in "who," for the pre-existense of the Person referred to, is contained in the verb "manifested." This could not be said of any mere man. Men are born, not manifested. Nor could it refer to the birth of an angel, for such a thing has never occured. Be that as it may, the fact that much, very much, can be said for the A.V. rendering, might well have sufficed to hinder the Revisers meddling with it. They were only authorised to correct "plain and clear errors," and a matter which has left so many scholars in doubt, can hardly be "plain and clear." The subject is fully discussed in that valuable work, Dean Burgon's " Revision Revised " (pp. 98-106. 424-501), a study of which conviced the well-known commentator, Dr. Christopher Wordsworth, who had previously championed " who," that " God," was indeed the true reading.

thy *holy one*" (Deut. xxxiii. 8). "He will keep the feet of His *saints*" (I Sam. ii. 9). "The Lord hath set apart him that is *godly* for Himself" (Psa. iv. 3). But no saint ever exhibited perfect godliness. Yet there are foreshadowings in the Old Testament of One who could be a perfect Servant, and righteously able to claim blessing on the ground of personal worth. In Isaiah i., the One who can "dry up the sea . . and clothe the heavens with blackness," is revealed as the fully obedient One, whose ear was opened, who was not rebellious, but who gave His back to the smiters . . and hid not His face from shame and spitting." In Psalm xxiv. also, we read of One who can claim to "ascend into the hill of the Lord" on the ground of "clean hands and a pure heart," and this One is "the King of Glory."

How this could be, remained a hidden mystery, until the One declared to be the Eternal God, the Creator of all things, in infinite grace became flesh, and dwelt among us (John i. 1-3, 14). This was indeed an unlooked for solution. That God should dwell on the earth in the Shekinah glory, was a marvel to Solomon (I King i. 17), how much more when He was manifested in the person of the meek and lowly One. It was in Him that "godliness" was fully exhibited ; as has been well said, "He was the source, power, and pattern of what is practically acceptable to God." His life in this scene was symbolized by the meat offering baked in the oven—spotless humanity passing through every fiery test and trial. A handful of this, with its oil and "all the frankincense" upon it, was

burnt upon the Brazen Altar "for a sweet savour,
even the memorial of it unto the Lord" (Lev. vi.
15)—fit figure of that precious memorial which the
earthly life of the Lord Jesus is to God.   This
manifestation of the Word was very real.   "He
became flesh, and dwelt among us."   His body was
real flesh and blood, not a spiritual body, but a true
human body.   And He Himself was a true manifestation of the moral glory of God.   He was the
image of the invisible God.   He that saw Him saw
the Father.   Seeing Him, we see the heart of God.
Divine holiness, grace, love, compassion shine out
brightly in all His ways.

None but God can fully know all that Christ's
manifestation entailed.   We have it presented to
us very fully in the well known Philippian passage.
He who was in "the form of God," whose mode of
existence was that of God, and who therefore *was*
God, determined in the fulfilment of the Divine
counsels not to insist on what had ever been His
undisputed right, to be equal and no less than equal
with God, but "made Himself of no reputation."
This last phrase does not mean that He ceased to
be a Divine Person.   He always and ever was that.
Nor yet that He divested Himself of His Divine
attributes, His omnipotence and omniscience for
instance, for then He must have ceased to be God.
But He held them in abeyance, retaining them to
the full, but never using them independently.   That
this is the true sense seems clear, from the explan-
atory words which follow, " but took upon Him the
form of a servant "—a new mode of existence which
He superadded to the former, without relinquishing

it. The special condition He assumed in order to
carry out this service was, not that of an archangel
—that would have been infinite condescension—but
that of man. He was "made in the *likeness* of men,"
yet only "in the likeness of sinful flesh" (Rom. viii.
3). Because, though truly man, He was morally
and intrinsically unlike fallen man. "And being
found in fashion as a man (that is, in outward
semblance in the "accidents "* of His being. seeming merely a man among men), He humbled Himself
and became obedient unto death, even the death
of the cross."

The path of perfect godliness meant the sacrifice
of all, and He made the sacrifice, but to the apparent
prejudice of all His claims.   He died as one
" numbered with the transgessors," forsaken of man
and of God.   Was ever apparent failure writ so
large on any mission? Certainly His manifestation
in the flesh and His atoning work had exposed
Him to misunderstanding and misapprehension.
He needed Divine vindication.   "God raised Him
up having loosed the pains of death, because it
was not possible that he should be holden of it "
(Acts ii. 24).   It is with this vindication, I would
submit, that the remainder of the verse is concerned.
He was "*Justified in the Spirit.*"†   The resurrection

* " The accidents " of a thing are the visible, tangible, ponder-
able qualities of the thing. Thus the "accidents of the bread and
wine" mean the colour, appearance, and weight of the elements.

† Some interpret " Spirit," of the Lord's human spirit or
" higher being," in order to make an antithesis between "in the
flesh " and in the Spirit," but the interpretation seems far-
fetched and hard of application.

by the power of the Holy Ghost (see Romans i. 4 ; viii. 11), was God's answer to a Christ-rejecting world. He who was disapproved of men, was approved by God as righteous.*

Not only so, but in resurrection He was vindicated before angelic hosts, "He was *seen of angels.*" They had seen Him made for a little "lower" than themselves, done to death, and engulfed in the tomb. They were the first to see Him on resurrection ground, as Conqueror of death and the grave.

Moreover, the very men who had at His death acknowledged themselves mistaken as to His Messianic claim, were so convinced by "many infallible proofs" of the reality of His resurrection, that they became His heralds, not only, as up till then, to the lost sheep of Israel, but to the uttermost ends of the earth He was "Preached *among the Gentiles.*" These heard with their ears what the angels had looked upon, and received the testimony, for He was "believed *on in the world*;" not, it is true, universally, for not yet does the knowledge of the Lord cover the earth as the waters cover the sea— that will only be at His return in power—but selectively, for there are already some who hear the call and acknowledge Him as Saviour and Lord, during His rejection. The crowning vindication

---

* " Justified " is used here in its usual tense in N.T. (see Luke vii. 29), a passage which shews that the meaning sometimes attributed to justified as "made righteous" is wholly inadmissible and erroneous. Justification is being *proved* righteous or *acquitted*. The justified man leaves the court, without a stain upon his character.

is reserved to the last, *not because last in order of time, but because greatest in order of value. He was "*Received up into glory*." Then the Lord's prayer was granted. He was glorified with the Father with the glory He had with Him, before the world was, awaiting the last supreme vindication when He shall be "revealed from heaven with His mighty angels, taking vengeance on them that know not God and that obey not the Gospel of our Lord Jesus Christ."

* The fact that the "preaching to the Gentiles" precedes in this verse "the ascension," surely shows that Alford's dictum that Paul is here following the "historical order of events," etc., is erroneous.

Chapter VI.

THE MYSTERY OF CHRIST.

THE mystery now before us, stamps a special character on the present dispensation, marking it off in the clearest manner from all that preceded or may follow it. It is designated in various ways in the Epistles. Paul calls it "The Mystery," as though to distinguish it from all the rest as *the* Mystery *par excellence*. "If ye have heard of the dispensation of the grace of God which is given me to you-ward, how that by revelation He made known unto me the Mystery" (Eph. iii. 3). It was by a special revelation that the apostle had become initiated unto this Mystery, in the same way, indeed, that he had also had communicated to him the great truths of the Gospel (1 Cor. xv. 3), the Lord's return for His saints (1 Thes. vi. 15), and the order of Lord's supper (1 Cor. xi. 23). And he tells us that, like the Mystery of Godliness, this also is a great Mystery' "This Mystery is great, but I speak concerning Christ and the Church" (Eph. v. 32). As far as we are directly concerned, it is of supreme importance, for it unfolds the deepest secret of the Divine counsels toward man. It is not surprising, when we discern its scope, that the apostle should count it a special grace to be the chosen instrument of its revelation. "Unto me who am less than the least of the saints is this grace given, that I should preach among the *Gentiles* the unsearchable riches of Christ ;" and not only so, but " to make *all men* see what is the fellowship of the Mystery." And then to a still wider range, "to the intent that *now* unto principalities and powers in heavenly places might be known by the church the manifold wisdom of God."

This Mystery is also termed the "Mystery of Christ " (Eph. iii. 4 ; Col. iv. 3), for though it deals with the body, the members cannot be separated from the Head, " from which all the body . . having nourishment ministered . . increaseth with the increase of God." And redemption is the base of it, for He who is the Head, the Centre, and Source of every blessing can only be so, because He was first the Redeemer. Then, again, this Mystery is called "the Mystery of the Gospel." "That I may open my mouth boldly to make known the Mystery of the Gospel " (Eph. vi. 19), for it is included in the Gospel and is its legitimate outcome. Any Gospel that does not eventually initiate souls into the enjoyment of the Mystery, is a defective Gospel. How often the horizon of believers is limited, not seldom because the horizon of preachers is so too, by forgiveness of sins, justification by faith (but little understood), a certain striving " to become better," and " do something for God," and a hope of " going to heaven when they die "! But is this all that is meant by "the unsearchable riches of Christ"? Does this exhaust the blessing of being "in Christ"? Had not the Old Testament saints

D

forgiveness of sins and justification by faith? (Gen. xv. ; Psa. xxxii.). Certainly they had, and knew the blessedness of them too, and we may truly say "there were giants in those days," compared with many of whom we are but pigmies. But still, our privileges are vastly greater. Not one in that great gallery of worthies whose names are given to us in Hebrews xi. had the most distant idea of the "Mystery of Christ," nor indeed had any share in it. The Spirit of God is careful to note that the Mystery was a new thing, "which in other ages was not made known unto the sons of men, as it is now revealed unto His holy apostles and prophets by the Spirit." The force of the word "as" is important. It marks, not a comparison of degree, as some have thought, but of fact. That is, it does not compare between a greater and less revelation, but between a full revelation in the Epistles and none at all in the Old Testament. This is clear from verse 9, "the Mystery that from the beginning of the world had been *hid in God*," or from Rom. xv. 25, where we learn that it was "*kept secret* since the world began," or, as in Col. i. 26, "*hid from ages* and from generations," and unrevealed* in the Old Testament. It is true there are incidents therein, such as the formation of Eve, the call of Rebecca, the marriage of Joseph, which serve to illustrate

---

* "The Song of Solomon" might seem to contradict this, but there it is the earthly bride, Israel, regarded as the married wife of Jehovah, whereas the Church is "betrothed to Christ." When this is seen, the "Song of Songs" remains as a beautiful expression of the affection of the individual believer to the Lord, in all dispensations.

what the Spirit of God is doing to-day in "calling out of the Gentiles a people for His Name." But the Church was non-existant till Pentecost, and the purpose of God regarding it was a secret.

The revelation of this Mystery was God's resource for man's failure. Man at his best, surrounded by every advantage, had been manifested in his true colours at the Cross. The Jew, and by inference, all men, were seen to be utterly ruined and irremediable. Man "under law," and man "without law" are total bankrupts. Blessing to Israel, and through her to the nations, must necessarily be postponed, in view of this national rejection of the Messiah. But must, therefore, God's purposes be altogether arrested? Nay, a divine counsel, more glorious than had ever been conceived, is now revealed in a new and altogether unexpected way of blessing to Jew and Gentile—the Church, the Body and the Bride of Christ. It was not, however, till the kingdom testimony had been definitely rejected by the elders of the nation, in imputing the signs of the kingdom to Beelzebub (Matt. ix. and xii.) that the Lord uttered the first hint of this in the memorable words, "On this rock I will build MY CHURCH."*

It is really quite arbitrary to assert, as some do, that "church" here means, not the Christian church,

* The word for Church (ecclesia) means "a called-out assembly." Thus Israel is called in one passage (Acts vii. 38), "the church in the wilderness," a suitable description, in that they had been called out of Egypt. But this must be carefully distinguished from the technical use of the word, as used in the Gospels, Acts, and Epistles.

but the Jewish assembly. Why should the Lord speak of building in the future what was already in existence? It is also quite illogical to affirm that " church " in the Acts is not the same as in the Epistles, on the ground, forsooth, that there is admittedly a " transitional " character in part of the Acts. Believers from Judaism were gradually weaned from their Jewish line of things to take up their heavenly character. Why should that alter the meaning of the " church," which was the very occasion of this transition?

No, the church the Lord spoke of was to be built at a later date ("I *will* build "), upon the foundation of the apostles and prophets (of New Testament times), Jesus Christ Himself—the Rock spoken of in Matt. xvi.—being the chief Corner Stone. In the Acts we see it historically, in its local and earthly aspect. It is not permissible to argue that because full church truth, as revealed in what some term "The Prison Epistles "—that is "The Ephesians," " Philipians," and "Colossians," written at the very close of the Acts period, was not fully revealed before, that therefore the church did not exist. Great Britain existed before "Magna Charta." The church was born at the beginning of the Acts, church truth at its close. The birth of the church, like that of Moses, was not fully revealed at first for obvious reasons, but even before Paul wrote the Ephesian Epistle (Acts xxviii. 30), he speaks at least four years before, in Romans xvi. 26, of the Mystery being "made known to all nations." Nor did Paul claim to be the only initiate, for he associates with himself "the holy apostles and prophets" (Eph.iii.5).

What then is the " Mystery of Christ ?" Certainly
not merely that blessing should come to Israel and
through them to the Gentile nations. Of this the
prophets are full, as such passages as Psalm lxvii.;
Isaiah lxvi. ; Amos ix., witness, the distinction
between Israel and the nations being maintained.
Israel was thus to be the head and the channel of
blessing, the Gentiles the tail and recipient thereof.
The Mystery is something quite different. *It reveals
that those called out of Israel and the Nations, should
be blessed together in one body and on equal terms.* It
has a threefold aspect as regards first the Gentiles,
then the church as a whole, and lastly, individual
believers.

First, the apostle Paul explains the Mystery in
perhaps the most unexpected aspect—as regards
the Gentiles. " That the Gentiles should be fellow-
heirs and of the same body. and partakers of his
promise in Christ by the Gospel " (Eph. iii. 6).
Nowadays, the conversion of Jews presents the
greatest difficulty to our minds, but in the early
days, when Israel at any rate still seemed to be the
favoured nation, the idea of Gentiles being blessed
on equal terms with her, appeared a thing indeed
hard to conceive. To accomplish this, four great
barriers had first to be removed. The high middle
wall of partition between Jew and Gentile had to
be broken down. The world was like a great
semi-detached house, inhabited by two lots of ten-
ants, Jew and Gentile, separated from one another,
at enmity with one another, and only united in one
point, their hatred of the Owner. First, then, that
which divided Jew from Gentile, and which con-

stituted the former "nigh" and the latter "afar off," was to be removed, for it must be remembered that the Jew had hitherto occupied the place of privilege. They were "a people near unto Him," whereas the Gentile was in a position of complete distance from God. The blood of Christ made the far-off Gentile nigh, without any intermediary stage of ceremonial nearness like the Jew. "Ye who once were far off (ye Gentiles), are made nigh by the blood of Christ." And the same blood availed for believing Israel. So that we read, "He is our peace who hath made both one. (Both what? Not peoples, that comes later ; but here the word is neuter, and refers to their positions Godward, "and hath broken down the middle wall of partition "*) (Eph. ii. 14).

But there is a second barrier to be considered. Not only were the two peoples positionally divided, but they were at "enmity," on account of "the law of commandments contained in ordinances." How could a Jew be reconciled to a Gentile whom he despised as uncircumcised, or a Gentile to a Jew, when he found himself shut out like a dog from the Passover and the other privileges of Israel ? Such a barrier could only be abolished by Christ, and He could only do it by His death. "Having abolished *in His flesh* the enmity, the law of commandments." Those who share in that death by faith, die to the law, and are reconciled on resurrection ground, where the law has no claim.

* This " wall of partition " was of God, and should suffice to shew that the Church position, where there is neither Jew nor Gentile, could not possibly have existed in Old Testament times.

But a yet more unsurmountable barrier would still remain—the enmity of Jew and Gentile to God. What could remove this barrier, but the supreme manifestation of the love of God in the Cross ? "That He might reconcile both (here it is both peoples, *i.e.*, believers from both) unto God in one body by the Cross, having slain the enmity thereby." "Reconciled to God by the death of His Son." "We love Him, because He first loved us."

But was nothing else required but that the sinner should be reconciled to God ? This might have satisfied man, but the Father's heart needed something more. He desired that the sinner should be brought as a purged worshipper to Himself. This too, is brought about by Christ. He "suffered once for sins, the Just for the unjust, that He might bring us to *God*." And He, too, is the Way of the worshipper to the *Father*. "No man cometh unto the Father but by Me." "Through Him we both (Jew and Gentile) have access by one Spirit unto the Father." Thus we see that in order that the purpose of "the Mystery" might be realised, peace must be proclaimed to Jew and Gentile, peace made between the two peoples, and then between them and God "by the blood of His Cross." We might call the Mystery from this point of view, "the Mystery of the Broken Barriers."

The Second view of the Mystery is that presented in chap. v., where it is not Jew or Gentile as such, but the whole church which is brought before us. "Christ loved the church and gave Himself for it." This is the love of election. God loved that mass of corruption—the world. That was His universal

love. Christ saw a pearl in that mass, loved it and
gave Himself for it, that having cleansed it by the
washing of water, that is by the once for all act of
regeneration—(the word for washing here, is the
root employed by our Lord in John xiii., "He that
is *bathed*")—He might sanctify it—nourishing and
cherishing it, while awaiting the day when He shall
present it to Himself "a glorious church, not having
a spot or wrinkle or any such thing." This is a
great Mystery, the apostle adds, " but I speak concerning Christ and the Church."

The last aspect of the Mystery to which reference
must be made, is the personal and experimental
side. "To whom God would make known what is
the riches of the glory of this Mystery among the
Gentiles, which is Christ in you the hope of glory."
Grammatically we might read "Christ among you,"
but this would be no mystery. But that the saints
should enter into such intimate spiritual union with
Christ, as to become part of Himself, and have Him
in the abundance of His resurrection life permeating
their very beings—a pledge of future glory, THAT
was indeed a mystery, worthy to be revealed to all
saints as a great fact, and to be enjoyed by each
(in a walk of holy separation from the flesh and
the world by simple faith). This Mystery then
unfolds the eternal purpose of God (Eph. v. 32), the
everlasting love of Christ (v. 25), the present
privileges and responsibilities of the believer (v. 27.
29), and his future glory and service (iii. 21).

·

Chapter VII.

THE MYSTERY OF GOD.

O F all the Divine Mysteries, none can be greater than this, for it is "the Mystery of GOD, even Christ,"* He who "in these last days" is the final revelation of God to man. Not that the Mystery is yet fully consumated. That will not be till the seventh trumpet of the Apocalypse has sounded, and the kingdoms of this world are transferred to their rightful King. "In the days of the voice of the seventh angel . . the Mystery of God should be finished, as He hath declared to His servants the prophets" (Rev. x. 7). That this declaration·had been concerning the kingdom glory of Christ is clear from chap. xi. 15, "And the seventh angel sounded, and there were great voices in heaven saying, The kingdoms of this world are become the kingdoms of our Lord and of His Christ, and He shall reign for ever and ever." When Christ returns, as the Son of Man, in the clouds, "every eye shall see Him," for His coming will be as the lightning, and His glory will fill the earth ; but now to those who have eyes to see, "the Mystery of God " is

---

* Of the many divergent readings in the MSS. of this passage, that adopted here is favoured by such scholars as Drs. Scrivener, and Lightfoot, and seems to correspond best with the rest of Scripture. It is important to note that Christ is not in oppositon to "God," but to "Mystery ; " and the meaning is the Mystery of God, which mystery is Christ.

revealed, "even Christ, in whom are hid all the treasures of wisdom and knowledge."* Some translate "in which," but "in whom" is better, for only a Divine Person can contain all fulness.

The circumstances of the Epistle to the Colossians are noteworthy. The condition of the saints, their faith and love (chap. i. 4), and their order and steadfastness (chap. ii. 5), called forth the thanksgiving of the apostle. But Satan was attacking their good condition, not openly by tempting to gross sin, but by sidetracking their faith. Moral evil is sure to follow doctrinal error. Doctrine is not human opinion, but the revelation of God's thoughts concerning Christ, man, sin, and atonement. The Colossians were in danger of being beguiled by philosophy and vain deceit and by the earthly principles of worldly religion. "Meat and drink, and holy-days,and new moons,and sabbaths" —the shadows, were obscuring Christ the reality. They were "not holding the Head." What a body is without a head, so is a Christian or a church, out of touch with Christ. What was the remedy? The only one that can ever set a Christian or a church right—Christ Himself. A serious feature of Satan's attack was, that his agents (like their

---

* As to the difference between "wisdom" and "knowledge," considered as human attributes, we may say, speaking generally that the latter is acquired in the schools of learning, the former in the school of experience. Knowledge without wisdom is pedantry. Knowledge stores up facts; wisdom turns them to profit. Wise men lay up knowledge and know how to use it aright (Prov. x. 17; xv. 2). Knowledge is theory. Wisdom practice. Knowledge tabulates diseases and remedies. Wisdom diagnoses and prescribes. Knowledge puffeth up; wisdom humbleth. As has been said, "We know that we all have knowledge; would that we knew that we have not all wisdom."

successors to-day, who quote much Hebrew and
Greek while often knowing but little) lay claim to
a special wisdom and an intuitive knowledge in
Divine things. They could talk of the "assured
results of the Higher Criticism," or of "the agreement of all scholars" with their own conclusions,
or what was the equivalent of these boasts in their
day. These pretentions beguiled the simple then,
as now. The apostle accordingly, in his deep con-
cern for them, prays that their hearts "might" be
comforted, being knit together in love, and unto all
riches of the full assurance of understanding (for
how much lack of comfort and spiritual understanding are breaches of fellowship responsible?) to the
acknowledgment of the Mystery of God, even
Christ, in whom are hid all the treasures of wisdom
and knowledge." Why should they "compass
themselves about with the sparks" of human
philosophy, when they had such resources of Divine
wisdom and knowledge in Christ, in whom the
Mystery of God is revealed.

God had in times past, made partial revelations
of Himself. In creation, His eternal power and
Godhead, as Elohim, were clearly seen. To the
patriarchs in their pilgrim journeys, He had made
Himself known as El-Shaddai,* the all-providing
God ; to Israel as Jehovah, the unchanging
covenant-keeping God. That there was a fuller
revelation still to come was an open secret. Prophets spake of a Child to be born who should bear

* Derived, as some believe, from Hebrew *shad*, a breast. It is
in this sense that I take it here. This interpretation enables us
to distinguish between Elohim and El-Shaddai, which is otherwise difficult.

the unheard of name of " God with us " (Isaiah vii.
14), of a Son who should receive the undreamt of
titles, " Wonderful, Counsellor, the Mighty God,
the Everlasting Father, the Prince of Peace "
(Isaiah ix. 6); of a coming ruler of Israel " whose
goings forth had been from of old, from everlasting."
Such words could only mean a revelation of God
in human form. Surely there would be no room
for doubt in face of such a manifestation. The
godly of the nation waited down the centuries, for
the fulfilment of the promise. And in "the fulness
of time, God sent forth His Son." And when He
came, there were some who were waiting for
redemption in Israel. Can it be that the long
expected promise is fulfilled in the babe of
Bethlehem, in the homeless Stranger of Galilee, in
the meek and lowly Jesus, the Man of Sorrows and
acquainted with grief, in the lonely rejected Man
of Calvary—crying out in the darkness, " My God,
My God! why hast Thou forsaken Me"? Yes, this
is "the Mystery of God, even Christ." And God
has attested it by raising Him from the dead and
giving "Him glory," that our faith and hope might
be in God." And "in Him are hid all the treasures
of wisdom and knowledge." He is at once the
Treasury, the Owner of the Treasure, and the
Treasurer.

Christ is *the Treasury*. He is the repository of all
the treasures of wisdom and knowledge ; "in Him
they are hid "—hid, that is, from the wise and
prudent, and also in the sense that they are
inexhaustible. There will always be more to know
than has ever been revealed.

¬ (2) He is also the *Owner of the Treasure*, for He possesses what He contains. He was omniscient in Incarnation, as before, being "the wisdom of God." The words in Philippians chap. ii. 7, " He made Himself of no reputation," are literally " He emptied Himself,"* and are expained by the words that immediately follow, "taking upon Him the form—or the mode of existence—of a servant." He did not divest Himself of His Divine attributes, but held them in abeyance : that is, He did not make independent use of them. He did not speak, act, or judge " from Himself," or on His own initiative. To continue to do so, would have been manifestly inconsistent with the position of a servant (Greek, *doulos*—a slave), which He had

---

* On these words, or rather on a misunderstanding of them, the Higher Critics have built up their theory of the *Kenosis* (the emptying), according to which our Lord entered into a condition down here in which he knew less of the Hebrew Scriptures and language and also of matters of fact than the Critics. But it may be questioned whether they really know as much as they claim. Has anyone who knows them been impressed to say to them, " Now we know that YE know all things ? " The words of our Lord in Mark xiii. 32, are the solitary proof adduced to the *Kenosis* theory. The words are omitted in some MSS., but their admitted difficulty favours their genuineness. We may be sure there is no contradiction in Scripture, and we must not allow one obscure verse to annul the general positive teaching of Scripture. The verse does not, as a matter of fact, limit the knowledge of Christ as " the Son of Man," but as the Son, and so goes further than the *Kenosis* theory. In the next verse, the Lord says, "Watch and pray for *ye* know not when the time is," so that His "not knowing the day " had nothing in common with their human ignorance. The statement, moreover, does not read like an admission of instrinsic limitation on our Lord's knowledge. Why was it that He " who knew the Father as the Father knew Him," was unaware of a day known to the Father, seems beyond our understanding. Clearly, it did not lead the apostles to doubt His omniscience when they said, " Now we are sure that Thou knowest all things," nor oblige the Lord to correct them with the proviso, " except the day of My coming."

voluntarily entered upon. That our Lord possessed nothing short of omniscience during "the days of His flesh," is clear to all who bow to the Scriptures. He claimed it in word, and proved it in deed. He knew from the beginning who they were that believed not, and who should betray Him. "One of you is a devil," He said to the twelve, at an early point in His ministry (John vi. 64, 70 ; xiii. 11), but He acted as though He did not know. He took men on their profession and reputation, and allowed them to manifest themselves in their own time. Judas was chosen as apostle, no doubt, on his public record as a disciple. Had he been omitted, the other disciples, it may be, would have thought an injustice had been done. This omniscience of our Lord in incarnation resulted naturally from what He had been before incarnation. He was the same personality as He had ever been. He claimed to know God in a way enjoyed by no one else. "No man knoweth the Father save the Son " (Matt xi. 27), and with the same absolute knowledge with which the Father knew Him. " As the Father knoweth Me, even so know I the Father " (John x. 15), and the word used here implies "accurate knowledge." To know the Infinite God accurately, includes all other knowledge, as the greater includes the less, and implies omniscience. The Lord enjoyed conscious knowledge not only of past time, " Before Abraham was I am " (John viii. 58), but of a past eternity. "Father glorify Thou Me with the glory which I had with Thee before the world was " (John xvii. 21). If he had forgotten nothing of a past eternity, surely His memory of past history was as good as that of the Critics who impugn Him!

In the Book of Isaiah, Jehovah attests His superiority over the idols of the heathen by His power to forecast the future. He challenges them to do the same. "I have declared the former things from the beginning . . let them bring them forth and shew us what shall happen ; let them shew the former things . . and shew the things that are to come hereafter, that we may know that ye are gods. . . Remember the former things of old, for I am God, and there is none else ; I am God, and there is none like Me, declaring the end from the beginning and from ancient times the things that are not yet done " (chaps. xlviii. 3; xli. 22; xli. 9, 10). This is the prerogative of God alone, and this power Christ claimed. He knew the future, not merely as a prophet by inspiration of God, but in Himself. He did not prelude His words with a "Thus saith the Lord," but with "Verily, verily, I say unto you," "MY words shall never pass away." He knew He would come in glory (Matt. xxvi. 64), that all would stand before Him to be judged (Matt. vii. 22 ; xxv. 31 ; John v. 22). He knew what the judged would say, and what He would reply (Luke xiii. 23). He knew all things that should come upon Him (John xviii. 4), and He knew He would reign in this scene of His rejection (Matt. xix. 28).

Again, in the Old Testament Scriptures, to read the heart is declared to be the prerogative of Jehovah. "I the Lord search the heart" (Jer. xxvii. 21). "The Lord searcheth all hearts and understandeth all the imaginations of the thoughts " (1 Chron. xxviii. 9). "The Lord looketh at the heart" (1 Sam. xvi. 7). To claim such knowledge is to claim omniscience, and nothing short of this was claimed for and by Christ. "He knew all men, and needed not that any should testify of man, for He knew what was in man" (John ii. 24, 25). " I know you, that ye have not the love of God in you" (John v. 42). "He knew in Himself that His disciples murmured" (John vi. 61). "He knew their thoughts" (Matt. xii.15; Luke vi. 8). "He knew they were desirous to ask Him" (John xvi. 19). One day "God will judge the secrets of men by Jesus Christ" (Rom. ii. 16), for all secrets are known to Him. In relation to His Manhood, the Lord could be said to be "full of wisdom," and yet to "increase in wisdom" (not knowledge) (Luke ii. 40, 52). In presence of the elder men, He acted as was seemly for a boy of twelve : " He heard them and asked them questions." But they soon made the discovery that they needed to ask Him questions, for we read, " All that heard were astonished at His under-standing and *answers*."

The reply of our Lord to Mary, shows that even at the early age of twelve, He had full consciousness of His Divine mission and of His heavenly relation-ships. This need not surprise us, as the same was true from conception (Psa. xxii. 9. 10). He was the " wisdom of God," but His wisdom was manifested along natural* lines.

* It is mere trifling, to adduce our Lord's silence as to the facts of astronomy and modern discovery, as a proof of His non-acquaintance with these facts. The mere pedant loves to display his knowledge to all, but " The prudent man concealeth knowledge" (Prov. xii. 23). The Lord's mission was not to hypnotise men with His knowledge of science and MMS., but to impart to them the knowledge of sin and of God.

The Lord's omniscience shines out in the records of His ministry. He knew Zaccheus and Peter by name, before He met them. He knew of the death of Lazarus before the news reached Him. He knew the past history of the Bethesda cripple and of the man born blind. Numberless instances could be adduced. He was acquainted with Nathaniel before Philip brought him to Him. The answer to his enquiry, " Whence knowest Thou me ? " convinced Nathaniel that He who had seen him when hidden from the eyes of man, could only be the Son of God. And guileless souls will never doubt the Deity of Him who knows them through and through. Could omniscience go further than our Lord's knowledge in the episode of the tribute money (Matt. xvii.. 27) ? He knew a certain fish had swallowed a piece of money. He left Peter free to go to the sea and cast his hook where he would. He knew that no other fish would take the hook, but that this very fish would be the first taken up. He knew the piece of money would be a stater, the very sum required, two didrachma, to pay the temple tax. One instance more may suffice : the incident of the search for a room where to observe the Passover. The Lord, in sending forth His disciples into the city, left them quite free to take their own road, but knew that by the way they would meet a man bearing a pitcher of water—a most unusual sight in an eastern city, where it is the woman's work to carry water—that the man would be going to the very house in which the owner had furnished and prepared, a large upper room, and that he would willingly place it at their disposal.

E

Again we may ask, could omniscience go further?

(3) He is also Himself *the Treasure*, for " it pleased all the fulness to dwell in Him." He was God's treasure, in whom His soul delighted. He is the wisdom of God, through whom all God's wisdom and knowledge are revealed, in Creation, Providence, and Redemption. " The Lord by wisdom hath founded the earth " (Pov. iii. 19). He was the " Wise Architect," who prepared the heavens (Prov.viii. 38, R.V.). He is the Creator of " all things that are in heaven and in earth, visible and invisible." Angelic hosts, the stellar universe, the spirit of man, "the springs* of the sea," the goodly† wings of the peacock," " the flower " of the field, the bones‡ of the behemoth, are but examples of His creative wisdom. The beneficent laws of Nature, the gifts of sun and rain, fruitful seasons, harvests, display His providential wisdom. Above all, the depths both of the riches of the wisdom and knowledge of God are seen, in His ways in redemption and grace, in "reconciling the world unto Himself." Christ " crucified " is unto them which are called, "the power of God and the wisdom of God," and proves that "the foolishness of God is wiser than man." God hath concluded them all (both Jew and Gentile) in unbelief that He might have mercy upon all," and it is His purpose that " now, uuto principalities and powers in heavenly places, might be know by the Church, the manifold wisdom of God."

(4) The Lord, too, is the *Treasurer*. He is the antitype of the treasurer, Eliakim (Isa. xxii. 22)—

* Job xxxviii. 16.   † Job xxxix. 13.   ‡ Job xi. 18.

the man whom God raised up, who was to bear on His shoulder the key of the House of David, "who openeth* and no man shutteth " not to the self-satisfied Laodiceans, but to the Philadelphians of "little strength," who had "kept His Word and had not denied His Name." It is the function of the Holy Spirit to unfold "the unsearchable riches of Christ " by means of the written Word. Christ does not so much give us wisdom, but "is made unto us wisdom, even righteousness, sanctification, and redemption." As a ray of light may be split up into light, heat, and chemical energy, so Divine wisdom is here seen resolved into its three constituents, by each of which is solved—an otherwise insoluble problem. Is the question, How can a guilty sinner be justified before a righteous God ? Christ is made unto us "righteousness " Is it, How can an unclean sinner be made fit for a Holy God? Christ is made unto us "sanctification." Or is it, How can a helpless sinner be delivered from the thraldom of sin and Satan ? Christ is made unto us "redemption." Christ does not give us stores of blessing and strength and wisdom, but He becomes to us moment by monent all that we need and trust Him to be, and becomes in very deed the provision of God to our souls.

* A comparison of Isaiah xxii. and Rev. iii. 7, seems to shew, that the opening referred to is primarily an opening of the treasury of God, revealing Christ in the Word to His humble people. To learn of the meek and lowly Teacher, the disciple should be meek and lowly.

Chapter VIII.

"MYSTERY, BABYLON THE GREAT."

LEAVING for later consideration the last of the Divine Mysteries, that of "Universal Headship" (Eph. i. 9, 10), let us turn to the solemn subject of what we may call the " Mysteries of Satan," namely "Mystery, Babylon the Great," and the "Mystery of Iniquity." These two consumations of evil, though sometimes confused, are really distinct, one being on the religious, the other on the worldly plane.

The Mysteries of God are, as we have seen, the unfoldings of His infinite resources in view of man's failures: the Mysteries of Satan are those failures in full development. If one who had seen the "Ecclesia," at the beginning of the present dispensation, in the first Springtide of her love and devotion, "betrothed to a chaste virgin to Christ," continuing "steadfastly in the apostles' doctrine and fellowship, and in breaking of bread, and prayers," and bearing a bright testimony to her absent and returning Lord, had fallen asleep, not for the twenty years of the legend, but for the whole course of the present age, what would be his horror on awakening to see in the place of professed testimony for God, no longer "a chaste virgin," but

an abandoned woman, bearing on her brazen fore-
head the name of infamy—"Mystery, Babylon the
Great, mother of harlots, and of abominations of the
earth?" What means this horrible portent, and
why is she called after Babylon, rather than after
Sodom, Tyre, or any other place prominent in Old
Testament history? Because of the relation which
historical Babylon bore to Israel, and the spiritual
significance of that relation. The countries brought
into contact with Israel in old time, seem to represent the world in its various phases of evil. Thus
Egypt would stand for the world in its ungodliness
and self-sufficiency. " The river is mine, and I have
made it " (Ezek. xxix. 9). Israel in Egypt corresponds with man in his unregenerate state. Tyre,
would represent the world in its commercial rivalries
and race for wealth (Ezek. xxvi. 2). What was it but
the spirit of Tyre that was behind the world war?
Edom is the world in its hatred of God's people
(Amos i. 4). Sodom, the world in its fleshy corruption, and Babylon, in its religious corruption
and persecution of the saints.

Israel was never again to return to Egypt as a
nation, but might and did fall under the power of
Babylon.

It is remarkable that the very king, through
whom God granted deliverance from the open
hostility of the Assyrian, was the first to fall under
the basilisk spell of Babylon, presenting herself as
friend and sympathiser, but how soon to rob his
treasury and lead his people captive. Babylon was,
in fact, the first great Gentile power to subjugate
the people of God, and is regarded as their greatest

enemy.   Satan always makes his most deadly attack first, and at the last goes back to it again.

Babylon was the beginning of the kingdom of Nimrod, the grandson of Ham, "the mighty hunter before the Lord" (Gen. x. 9), a hunter, surely, of nobler quarry than mere beasts, of "the bodies and souls of men " (see Rev. xviii.13, marg.).   From the words, "He began to be mighty on the earth," we may gather that he was a successful conqueror. Not only so, but he was a mighty leader against God, for comparing this passage with the account of the building of Babel and its tower in chap. xi., we see that he was the Great Initiator,* the brain of that tremendous undertaking which marked the first confederate departure from God since the flood ; but the confederation ended in confusion† and dispersion, as all man-made associations must. "Associate yourselves, and ye shall be broken to pieces."   "Union is strength" only when it is a union which is of God and with God.   "United we fall " may serve as a motto for world-leaguers and alliance-mongers.

Nothing is said of the destruction of the tower of Babel, and there seems no doubt it became later the great temple of Belus, or Bel‡, the mighty lord,

* Nimrod is represented by tradition as a black man with an enormous head, very ugly, and lame.   He was evidently the architype of the fire gods of Greek and Roman Mythology, Hephaistos and Vulcan, who were deformed monsters and lame to boot, and is no doubt the forerunner of the last great leader against God, that is to be, the Man of Sin.   It is remarkable that Bel was a title attached to his name, Satan thus associating with himself this evil man.

† Babel, from a Hebrew root, signifying, "to confound."

‡ Our Lord recognised Beelzebub (the lord of flies of Ekron) as none other than Satan.

rival of the Lord of Lords. This temple was half a mile in circumference and 660 feet in height, loftier than the Great Pyramid. It was constructed in eight successive towers, gradually decreasing in width, and surmounted by a golden statue, 40 feet high.

It is remarkable that Arabs call the immense mound, which to-day marks the ruin of the tower, Birs Nimroud, thus marking its identity with its founder. Even if it cannot be proved that Nimrod claimed divine honours in his lifetime, he certainly was deified* after his death. Babylon was a centre of idolatry, and "Satan's seat" in a special degree. Thus it posed as the rival and opponent of Jerusalem, where was Jehovah's throne, "between the cherubim." The judgment of God, fell on Babylon, not only because of the evil she had worked against Jerusalem (Jer. li. 34), but first and foremost on account of her shameless idolatries. "Babylon is fallen, is fallen; and all the graven images of her gods He hath broken unto the ground" (Isa. xxi. 9). "Two things shall come to thee in a moment . . the loss of children and widowhood . . for the multitude of thy sorceries and for the great abundance of thine enchantments" (Isa. xlvii. 9). "A sword is upon . . the inhabitants of Babylon . . for it is the land of graven images, they are mad upon their idols" (Jer. l. 25, 38). All idolatry is addressed to some demon, "for the things which the Gentiles sacrifice they sacrifice to demons and not to God;" and that of Babylon was to Bel, the prince of the demons.

* "The Two Babylons," by Hyslop.

Israel, by her departure from God to Baal, made it necessary for God in righteousness to hand them over to Babylon. It was fitting that their bodies should be carried where their hearts had already wandered. To-day, when we see the feet of professed believers turned again to Babylon, we know that they have trod the path in heart before.

Babylon was built on both sides of the Euphrates in an immense square, of at the lowest computation, 34 miles in circumference (Herodotus made it 60 miles), of $8\frac{1}{2}$ miles to each side. The river was spanned by a great bridge of stone, clamped with iron and roofed over, which connected the two parts of the city, but of which no trace remains to-day. The temple of Belus was in the western city ; the Hanging Gardens, built by Queen Semiramis on successive tiers of arches, up to the height of the walls, were on the eastern side of the river. There was a moat of running water around the city, and the walls, pierced for a hundred gates of solid brass, were at least 300 feet high and 70 feet broad, surmounted by a street on which a chariot of four horses could easily turn. Of all these enormous walls, the greatest known in the history of the world, nothing is seen to-day, though when the prophecies were uttered fortelling her utter ruin, nothing could have seemed less probable than such a catastrophe. But no word of God can fall to the ground. Isaiah prophesied more than 165 years prior to the taking of Babylon and 200 before Herodotus, "the father of history," as the world calls him, and yet the prophet not only names the man destined by God to be the first to humble

Babylon, but describes the manner of its capture. Cyrus accomplished this in 538 B.C., after more than two years' siege, by turning aside, as is well known, the course of the Euphrates. It was taken a second time by Darius Hystaspes in 516 B.C., and later on by Alexander the Great. Through centuries, the great city declined, until the prophecies were literally fulfilled, the broad walls of Babylon were " utterly broken," and she herself " became heaps."

Some students of prophecy believe that Babylon must be rebuilt, on the ground that two or three specific details named in the prophecies have not been fulfilled in the destruction that has already taken place. I think a more careful reading of the prophecies goes to shew that such an idea is mistaken.

Let us examine the supposed discrepances. Does it not say, it is objected, that the judgment of Babylon should come upon her suddenly, which she should not know? (Isa. xlvii. 11). How reconcile this with centuries of decline and decay ? The words of the prophet may quite well mean that she should be taken by surprise, as indeed she was. Her judgment was to come upon her suddenly, but it does not say it was to be finished suddenly. But then does not Isaiah xiii. 19 distinctly say that " Babylon . . shall be as when God overthrew Sodom and Gomorrha : it shall never be inhabited, neither shall it be dwelt in from generation to generation ? " Yes, the *result* would be the same in both cases. Babylon, like Sodom and Gomorrha, should *not be inhabited*, but it does not say that the *manner* of their judgment should be the same (see also Jer. l. 40). That Hillah, an Arab town of some importance, exists to-day in the neighbourhood, does not negative this, as it remains to be proved that this place is within the site of the ancient Babylon. The fact that in its gardens there are said to be no traces of ruins would rather point to the contrary. But again does it not say that no stone shall be taken from Babylon to build with, and is it not well known that neighbouring cities were built from her bricks? This last fact is so, but it is not accurate to apply the words to Jer. li. 25, 26, to Babylon as a whole. They are addressed to "the destroying mountain," now named "Birs Nimroud." "They shall not take of thee a stone for a corner nor a stone for a foundation." This has been literally fulfilled. The great mound of ruins is truly a " burnt mountain "—vitrified by a judgment of fire, and is thus quite unfit to produce either corner or foundation stones.

The idea that Babylon must be rebuilt is not only far-fetched and mistaken,* but introduces confusion into the description of the woman's seat in Rev. xvii. 9, 18. The city on which she rests is built, we are told, on several mountains, and was, when the apostle wrote, "reigning over the kings of the earth." This was certainly not true then of Babylon, nor do seven hills exist in the plain of Shinar, on which the literal city of Babylon could be rebuilt. We have one city which corresponds with this twofold description, and we need no other.

* The reader is recommended to read " Keith on Prophecy" (to which the present writer owes much information', if he would be convinced that the prophecies against Babylon have been literally and adequately fulfilled,

But when it is affirmed that the prophecies against Babylon have been so literally fulfilled as to render needless any further rebuilding of the historical city, it is not meant that these prophecies have been exhausted. There is a "fulfilment" still to come, as we shall now see.

For centuries, Babylon had only been an immense historical reminiscence and nothing more,* a title to be conferred half in flattery, half in reprobation on one or another of the great modern capitals of Christendom, when suddenly the Prophetic Word presents her to us as an actual reality. "Great Babylon," we read, "came in remembrance before God to give unto her the fierceness of his wrath" (Rev. xvi. 19). "Babylon the great is fallen, is fallen" (Rev. xviii. 7). But how can that fall which has already fallen, or that be judged which has been destroyed? Only by having once more come into existence under a new guise. Satan will end where he began. It was, indeed, a crushing, personal reverse for him when Babylon was razed to the ground. "Bel was confounded." He found himself without a seat, and obliged to seek a new sphere, wherein to carry out the old policy. Here we see the malignant subtlety of Satan toward the Eve of the New Creation. Persecution had but fanned her faith, might not favour quench it? We know too well how he succeeded in his effort, and what the result has been.

Literal Babylon represents a *city*, the capital of the first great Gentile power, the centre of an

* The Babylon where Peter wrote his First Epistle, was probably a small town in Egypt.

idolatrous *system* centred in a city, the capital of
the last great Gentile power.   One of the seven
angels, who had just poured out the vials of God's
wrath, is commissioned, in the 17th of Revelation,
to shew John the judgment of the great whore, just
as later to display the glory of the Bride.   The
"great whore" is referred to in verse 1 as "seated
upon many waters," explained in verse 15 to mean
"peoples and multitudes and nations and tongues."
This describes her characteristic position for centuries past, the world-wide scope of her spiritual
empire.   But the special position in which the
angel displays her to John is as "seated upon a
scarlet-coloured beast."   The preposition "upon"
is the same in both places, but in verse 3 it governs
a case, denoting motion *on to*.   She has clambered
up on to the beast.   At last she has realised her
secular ambitions, and is seen in the zenith of her
power—prelude to her everlasting abasement.   A
rider not only rides, but guides his steed.   So the
woman is seated on the beast and "reigns over the
kings of the earth."   It matters nothing that the
beast is "full of the names of blasphemy."   Eccles-
iastical corruption is profoundly indifferent to
Christian principle.   Spiritual life and separation
from the world are immaterial ; position, wealth,
talent are indispensible.   Does not she herself
flaunt the shameless name—"Mystery, Babylon the
Great, mother of harlots and of the abominations
of the earth " ?   This sub-title "mother of harlots,"
is expressive of the true scope of Babylon.   Just as
"Babylon " of old days described often more than
the city, so "Mystery Babylon " has daughters,

harlots like herself, perhaps in externals diverse, in essentials certainly the same. The scarlet-coloured beast represents the Roman world in its last phase, but the fact that the ten horns are not crowned, would shew, that the scene before us precedes the "hour" in which the ten kings will receive power as *kings* with "the beast" (chap. xvii. 12).

The woman is arrayed in purple and scarlet costume, thus rivalling by imitation the regal glory of the world, and is decked (*lit.* gilded) with gold and precious stones and pearls, in contrast with that which "becometh women professing godliness, good works" (I Tim. ii. 9, 10).

She holds a golden cup in her hand, travesty of the cup of salvation, and "full," not of joy and communion, but of abominations and filthiness. She is viewed, not as Israel of old as an adulteress, but as is proper for one who counterfeits the affianced bride, as an abandoned woman, committing fornication with the kings of the earth, and making the people drunk with the wine of her fornication. The great ones of the earth are not deceived, policy alone shapes their ends. But the vulgar crowd is deceived—intoxicated with her religious displays, art, music, oratory and millinery, as they are by operatic scenes or theatrical shows. And she is intoxicated herself. Instead of being "filled with the Spirit," she is "drunk with the blood of the saints, and with the blood of the martyrs of Jesus." But her triumph is short ; her judgment lingereth not. It will fall first on the System by the hand of man (see chap. xvii. 16), and later on the City from the hand of God (chap. xvi. 19).

Chapter IX.

"THE MYSTERY OF INIQUITY."

THE destruction of Babylon, the corrupt religious system, will make room for something even worse, the "Mystery of Iniquity." The same process is being enacted to-day in Papist countries, like France and Portugal, where a corrupted faith has practically given place to no faith. In such lands there is a certain liberty of indifference, which allows wide distribution of "Gospels," but hearts open to the Gospel are but few. It will be when the Mystery of Iniquity is revealed, that "God shall send men a strong delusion that they may believe a (lit., the) lie." But this will not be till long after the coming of the Lord for His Church. Between that event and this delusion, will have occurred times of blessing, probably without parallel before in the history of the world. If Satan rises up against himself and destroys Babylon, it will be because she will have served his purpose long enough. He will have not a moment to lose "for he knoweth that he hath but a short time" "The Mystery of Iniquity" will be the climax of lawlessness*—when "iniquity shall have come to the full." The promise of Eden will then be consummated. It seemed such a trifling thing to

* Iniquity in 2 Thess. ii. 7 ought to be translated "lawlessness." So also in verse 8, "that wicked" should be translated "that lawless."

take the forbidden fruit. Really, it was man setting up to be God on his own account, as every act of self-will is in principle to-day. "The Mystery of Iniquity" is the unexpected consummation of this. Lawlessness had been an age-long fruit of sin: there is nothing new in that. Men like Nimrod, as we have seen, had been deified after their death. The "Mystery" was already working in the apostles' time. The Roman Emperors, some of them, were deified in their life time. The "New Theology" pretends that man is divine, but who would have imagined that a man could claim to be the only God. We see things working up to a general revolt against all authority in the home, in the nation, and alas! in the churches. Trade Unionism, Socialism, Syndicalism, and kindred godless movements will find an articulate cry in the words, "Let us break their bands asunder, and cast away their cords from us." All is tending toward two great events, "The Mystery of Lawlessness," and then the "Mystery of His Will." But Israel must first be restored to the place of testimony. The true Pentecost of Joel will prepare her for this. Her testimony will be the Gospel of the Kingdom—"The King is coming!" Multitudes of all flesh will be saved, but it is easy to imagine how intolerable such a testimony will be to the ungodly world of those days, and Satan will prepare his counterblast, "The King *has* come!" and the counterfeit God-man will be presented to an astonished world with the credentials of "all power and signs and lying wonders," in the person of the Man of Sin, the first beast of Revelation xiii. His claims will be sustained with Satanic power by the second beast, the Antichrist, the false Messiah and King of Israel. These two super-men will form with the Dragon, who inspires them, the Satanic Triad of the last days, a counterfeit of the Trinity.   The Dragon once had the highest place of any creature. "Perfect in beauty," "full of wisdom," he "sealed up the sum." He was "the anointed cherub that covered" (Ezek. xxviii.), but not content with this, he aimed at the throne of God.   "I will exalt my throne above the stars. . . I will be like the Most High" (Isa. xiv. 13, 14).   The greatest tragedy in the universe is a Cherub turned Dragon.   The Man of Sin will arise out of the revived Roman Empire as the little horn of Daniel vii.   Nebuchadnezzar, in his dream, saw four Gentile empires, to whom God intended to entrust the kingdom during the national dethronement of Israel, Babylon, Medo-Persia, Greece, and Rome, represented in their official glory by four metals—gold, silver, brass, and iron, decreasing in value as they recede from the Divine ideal of absolute monarchy.   An element of weakness is introduced in the feet—the clay—the democratic socialistic element.   In chap. vii. the same empires are seen in their moral degradation as four wild beasts—a lion, a bear, a leopard, and a nameless monster, and these decrease in nobility and increase in ferocity.   All attempts to form a fifth world empire have failed,* and must fail, for

*The Carthagenians, Moors, Turks, have all come near this, but have failed. The Germans seem to be making another attempt in the present war. Were they to succeed, which they cannot, a fifth world-empire, outside the old Roman Empire, would arise on the ruins of the British and French Empire, which form part of it.

the fifth is "the Kingdom of God and of His Christ."

In his vision, Daniel saw the fourth empire as it will be under the ten horns, and therefore in its last stage of developement. He describes the rise of "the little horn," which overthrows three of the ten. In Rev. xiii. the beast is seen with seven heads as well as ten horns, of which one is wounded to death, is healed, and becomes eventually the eighth or last great Ruler of the revived Roman Empire. The eighth head and the little horn are therefore identical, though in one extraordinary point they will not be. This we shall see later. Let us turn now for a moment to Revelation xiii. The opening words, as is well known, ought to be, "And he (i.e., the dragon) stood upon the sand of the sea shore." Then follows the rise of the great beast, which we have little difficulty in recognising as the fourth beast of Daniel. It embodies traits of three previous empires—the leopard, the bear, and the lion ; truly a monster "dreadful and terrible," having, as we have seen, " seven heads and ten horns, and upon his horns ten crowns, and upon his heads the name of blasphemy . . and the dragon gave him his (i.e., his own) power and his seat and great author-ity," and then the apostle adds—" I saw one of his heads as it were wounded to death, and his deadly wound was healed " (Rev. xiii. 1-3). The wounding and miraculous recovery of this head is well worth our close attention. In Rev. i. the Lord describes Himself as " He that liveth and was dead and is alive for evermore." Throughout the Book, this is characteristic of the Lamb. He has been " slain " (e.g.. see chap. v. 6) but is now alive. This word "slain" is the sacrificial word, and is identical with that used of the wounded head of the Beast "*wounded* to death"—the word "as it were" is simply the word translated in chap. v. "*as it had been* slain." The head will be truly slain and brought to life by Satanic power—a travesty of the resurrection. This marvel seems to be realised in a double way. The then ruler of the Roman Empire will be wounded to death and miraculously healed. But previously, perhaps centuries before, one of the seven heads of the beast will have been slain with a sword, and his spirit, instead of going to Hades, the usual abode of the wicked dead, will have been preserved in the bottomless pit or abyss —the very place Satan will be shut up in during the millennium. The first thing, indeed, we hear of the beast in his personal character is, that he will "ascend out of the bottomless pit," and make war against God's two witnesses, and will overcome them and kill them (chap. xi. 7.) These two, the present and past rulers, will become in some way mysteriously combined. May it not be, I would suggest, that the wicked spirit of the past "head" will come out of the abyss and take possession of the body of the then present ruler, who had received the deadly wound. It this be so, the dead one will come to life again energized by the spirit of a past Roman Emperor, destined thus to play a second rôle in this world's affairs. The electrifying bulletin will circle the globe. "The deadly wound is healed." A miracle has been performed by the Dragon's power, and men will worship him, as the Great Lifegiver. "The Man of Sin " will thus be a dual personality with super-human powers, and he will be an object of almost universal worship.

The first beast of Revelation xiii. is said to rise out of the sea, *i.e.*, the Mediterranean, as the direct result of the presence of Satan on the earth. It is very important to notice that this beast represents first a system, the Roman Empire revived ; then, after the wounding and healing of one of its seven heads, the system personified in that head, a Roman Emperor revived. This distinction has been over-looked, and confusion has been the result. The first beast is interpreted accordingly, meaning only the Roman Empire, and the second beast the Human Person, or the Man of Sin and the Anti-christ rolled into one. That the first beast ends as a Human Person is clear from chaps. xi. 7 and xvii. 8, where he is said to "ascend out of the bottomless pit." this could not be said of a system, whereas it is quite intelligible, if we allow that "the Man of Sin " will have already lived on the earth, died, and is brought back to this scene at a later date. Then, again, in chap. xvii. we read, "The beast that was and is not, even he is the eighth (head or king), and is of the seven, and goeth into perdition." Here the beast is personified in the eighth head, who will prove to be one of the previous seven raised to life again. Chap. xiii. 18 is even clearer, "Let him that hath understanding count the number of *a man*,* and his number is 666." This refers to

* An attempt has been made to explain this number 666, as referring to the duration of the empires represented in Nebu-chadnezzar's image. But is there any other instance in the New Testament of a period denoted by the values of the Greek letters?

the first beast, of whom the second beast makes an image.

The seven heads and ten horns are interpreted in either case as kings.* Thus we read in chap. xvii. 10 of the heads, "There are seven kings, five are fallen, and one is, and the other is not yet come, and when he cometh he must continue a short space." This last phrase excludes the Papacy, for that has continued nearly 1500 years.

John was told, "The ten horns which thou sawest are ten kings, which have received no kingdom as yet, but receive power as kings one hour with the beast" (chap. xvii. 12). How then, if "heads" and "horns" both mean "kings," are we to distinguish them? The "heads" are successive (though not necessarily consecutive), the "horns" contemporaneous. The seven heads will have reigned during the first phase of the Roman Empire, the "horns" will reign after its revival, during its final phase. Not that the same geographical area will necessarily be rigidly adhered to, but the same parts of the earth will be represented, though the powers in question may have Colonies and possessions outside the limits of the old empire. Britain, France, Spain,

* The heads also mean "seven mountains on which the woman sitteth" (chap. xvii. 9). The woman is therefore Rome, "the city of the seven hills," as she is known in history, "that great city which," when John was writing, "reigned over the kings of the earth." Whether Babylon be rebuilt or no, is not in my judgment a matter which touches this prophecy, for when John was writing, by no stretch of imagination could she be said to be built on seven mountains, or to be "reigning." The seven heads are sometimes interpreted as seven forms of government which have existed in the Roman State from its beginning, but this overlooks the fact that the beast represents Imperial Rome, in which only one form of Government is possible.

Portugal, and Italy may prove to be the western horns, and Greece, Serbia, Roumania, Montenegro, and some Syrian kingdom the eastern. Their reign will be brief, "one hour with the beast." We may connect this expression "one hour" with that in I John ii. 18, "the last hour,etc.," to be characterised by the presence of Antichrist. In Psalm lxxxiii. the subject is a confederacy against Jehovah and against Israel, " The tabernacles of Edom, and the Ishmaelites ; of Moab, and the Hagarenes ; Gebal and Ammon and Amalek ; the Philistines with the inhabitants of Tyre ; Asshur also is found with them." Ten peoples are enumerated here. May not these be the nations whose representatives are known to-day as the southern nations of Europe ? Their object will be to cut them off (*i.e.*, the hidden ones of Jehovah) from being a nation, that the name of Israel may be no more in remembrance (v. 4). And this will be the aim of the nations gathered together against Jerusalem in the last days (Joel iii. 2 ; Zech. xiii. 7, 8 ; xiv. 2). But they will themselves be cut off, and then it will be true of their survivors, that "ten men shall take hold out of all languages of the nations (one from each) even shall take hold of the skirt of him that is a Jew, saying, We will go with you, for we have heard that God is with you " (Zech. viii. 23). Then, too, they will have to confess, " The Lord hath done great things for them."

The Man of Sin is not the Antichrist, though he too, will claim divine honour. God only recognises one building on earth as His temple, and that is the temple at Jerusalem. There, in the holy place, the Man of Sin will impiously take his seat as God. When not there personally, it seems likely that he will be replaced by the mysterious image—the synthetic man—which the Antichrist will produce by Satanic power. This will prove to be the "abomination of desolation spoken of by Daniel the prophet" ("abomination" is a well-understood phrase in Scripture for an idol). That is to be the signal to all faithful Jews for their immediate flight to the mountains, from the tribulation which must then ensue. The "Man of Sin" will make extraordinary claims, but will also offer extraordinary credentials calculated to test the faith, even of the elect (Matt. xxiv. 24, R.V.). The first appearance of this terrible leader against God and His people, will be as "a little horn," arising among the ten horns of the fourth beast of Daniel (see chap. vii.). He will overthrow three of them, and the others will recognise the *fait accompli* and hail him as the Man of Destiny, qualified to lead the great confederacy.

Consummate Generalship, then will be the first credential of this Man of Sin. The second will be his *Mysterious Recovery* from "the deadly wound" by Satanic power, which will cause men to worship him. This effect will be heightened by his *Superhuman Victory* over the two witnesses. What greater proof of divine power than to slay the witnesses of God, who, till then, had slain all their foes? This victory will succeed his *Supernatural Resurrection* from the bottomless pit. It is as the beast that ascended "out of the bottomless pit" that he shall make war on the two witnesses and overcome them and kill them. He will further receive *Miraculous Attestation.* Not only will his coming be "after the working of Satan with all power and signs and lying wonders," but his claims will be supported by the Antichrist, who will "exercise all the power of the first beast before him, and cause the earth . . to worship the first beast 'whose deadly wound was healed ' . . and do great wonders, so that he maketh fire come down from heaven on the earth in the sight of men."

Never will there have been such a being on the earth before, backed by all the power* of Satan, entrusted by men with all their powers, and having also power from God to continue forty and two months (chap. xiii. 4, 7; xvii. 13). Then it will be, when the Man of Sin is fully manifested, that God shall send men a strong delusion, that they should believe THE lie, that they all might be damned, who believed not the truth, but had pleasure in un- righteousness " (2 Thess. ii. 12). All will worship him, whose names are not written in the Book of Life of the Lamb slain, from the foundation of the world (chap. xiii. 8).

The coming of the Lord *for* His saints is not governed by dates, nor does it depend on historical or political events. With God's earthly people, it is different. Scripture shows, that before a "cov- enant" with Israel as a nation is possible, they must not only have been restored, at least in part, to their own land, but their land must have been restored to them.

This covenant will be the recognition by the

---

* It is the same word *excousia*—authority—in all three cases.

Powers, of their national existence under their king —the one who will "come in his own name" (John v. 43), and whom Israel will receive. He must be a Jew, for it is unthinkable that the nation would accept anyone else as their Messiah. This is the second beast of Rev. xiii., who will arise out of the land—that is, the land of Palestine. He will in appearance be for God, having "two horns like a lamb," but will be possessed of Satan, for he will speak "like a dragon." He will doubtless further "the covenant" between Israel and the great Emperor of the Roman alliance—a covenant which will probably guarantee to the nation their national rights and religious freedom, but to the Spirit of God it will be "a covenant with death and an agreement with hell."

Two things will hold good during the first half of the week. The city, except certain portions, shall be "trodden down by the Gentiles," which means, I would suggest, that the city will be held in force, as in the modern case of Crete, by detachments of the troops of the ten kingdoms, to guarantee the inviolability of the holy places which could not be left in the hands of the Jews. During the same three and a half years, the two witnesses, probably Moses and Elias (not Enoch, for he was not of Israel, and could hardly take part in a Jewish testimony), will deliver their testimony, backed up by miraculous power. They, too, will be men brought back from the other world to live and act once more in this scene. When they shall have finished their testimony, "the beast that ascendeth out of the bottomless pit (the Man of Sin) shall make war

against them, and shall overcome them and kill
them." This will be the occasion for his full
manifestation, and also for that of the Antichrist.
"In the midst of the week, "when the Roman
Emperor, the Man of Sin, will tear up the covenant
like another 'scrap of paper,'" and cause "the
sacrifice, the oblation, to cease; he will have the full
support of the false King of Israel. Henceforth they
will come forward as the avowed rivals and enemies
of God and His Christ, for whose worship will be
substituted that of the Beast and his image. The
bulk of the nation will follow their king. The unclean spirit will come back to the nation and find
it "empty, swept and garnished," and they will
plunge into an idolatry such as was never known
before, and their last end will be worse than the first.

So Satan's false Christ will combine a claim to
Messiahship with the office of False Prophet. The
way "*the* false prophet " is introduced in Rev. xix.
as "the false prophet that did miracles before the
beast," clearly points us to the second beast of
chap. xiii., and leaves no reasonable room for doubt
as to their identity. The relation between the
second beast and the first is that of prophet and
god. Between them, the Name of God will be
banned in the earth. All open human testimony
will be impossible. This will be the day of Jacob's
trouble—the Great Tribulation of the Gospels. It
will occupy the second half* of the 70th week.

* The second half of the week will not, it would seem, reach
its proper completion. "Except those days should be shortened,
there should no flesh be saved: but for the elect's sake those
days shall be shortened" (Matt. xxiv. 22). In Daniel viii. 13,
the question is asked, "How long shall be the vision concerning

The victory of Satan will appear complete.   But his seeming victories are the times of his defeats. The two Arch-Rebels will be summarily dealt with. There will be no need that they should be judged before the Great White Throne.   Their cup of iniquity will be not only full but overflowing, and their heinous guilt will be manifest to the universe. They will be cast alive into the lake of fire. . Two men in the Old Testament went to heaven without dying.* Two in the New, will go to hell without seeing death.   The first to enter that fearful place of everlasting torment, "prepared for the devil and his angels," will be two men, a Gentile and a Jew. Thus will the Mystery of Iniquity be unmasked and undone for ever, to make room for the manifestation of the " Mystery of His Will."

the daily sacrifice . . . to give both the sanctuary and the host to be trodden underfoot? and He said unto me, Unto 2300 days; then shall the sancutary be cleansed." 2300 days, is 220 days short of 7 years. The first half of " the week " will have run its full, the second will apparently be shortened by over 7 months.

* The question is sometimes asked, whether such and such a wicked ruler is the "Antichrist " or the " Man of Sin ? "   No doubt Satan has had his types of these men, like Nimrod. Rameses ii., Antiochus, Epiphanes, Caligula, etc., but the Antitypes cannot be recognised until certain events above referred to, occur, though it is not impossible that both these terrible men of destiny, are alive on the earth to-day.

Chapter X.

"THE MYSTERY OF HIS WILL."

IT is with relief that we turn once more from the Mysteries of Babylon and of Iniquity to the Mysteries of God. The former are the short-lived pseudo-triumphs of Satan; the latter will fill the eternal ages. God has revealed one more mystery, "the Mystery of His will." "That in the dispensation of the fulness of times He might gather together in one all things in Christ, both which are in heaven, and which are in earth, even in Him" (Eph. i. 10). It is fitting to consider this last in the series of mysteries, for it is bound up with the eternal glories of Christ and nothing can supersede it. The word translated " gather-together-in-one" would be more accurately rendered, "head up." It only occurs in one other place in the New Testament (Rom. xiii. 9), and is there translated " briefly comprehended," or, as we say, "summed up." We may compare this with the word in Ezekiel xxviii. 12, in the lamentation of Jehovah over the King of Tyre, who can be none other than Satan, " Thou sealest up the sum," or, as the French version has it, "Thou art the crown of the edifice." As Adam was the masterpiece and head of an earthly creation, so it would appear was Satan of the heavenly. But it was God's purpose to take this place Himself in the Person of the Son. Indications are not wanting (though it would be unwise to dogmatise) that the test of angelic obedience was the acknowledgment of the Headship of the Son to be manifested in a created form of a lower order than their own. This may be referred to in Heb. i. 6, "And again when he bringeth (or in literal order—"when again he bringeth") the First-begotten into the world, He saith, And let all the angels of God worship Him."* This would account for the special hatred of Satan to Christ "the Firstborn," and to the "many sons" whom Christ is bringing to glory through Him, in whom they also have "obtained an inheritance" (Eph. i. 11). When Satan fell, through exalting himself, the universe was, as it were, a pyramid without a headstone of the corner. This place is reserved for Him "who, being in the form of God . . humbled Himself and became obedient unto death, even the death of the Cross." As Satan's degradation is in stages (see Ezekiel xxviii. 19-18), so is the elevation of Jesus Christ. Already has God "highly exalted Him," and given Him the Name which is above every name (that is the name of Lord in view of a future exaltation), that at the name of Jesus (not at the name "Jesus," but His full title, "the Lord Jesus") every knee should bow, of things in heaven, of things in earth, and of

* This is usually referred to as a quotation from Psa. xcvii. 7. " Worship Him all ye gods," but it is remarkable that the exact words, as quoted in Heb. i. 6, are found in the Septuagint Version of Deut. xxxii. 43, from which it would seem clear that they existed in the Hebrew manuscript from which that translation was made.

things under the earth ; and that every tongue should confess that Jesus Christ is Lord to the glory of God the Father " (Phil. ii. 9-11). In other words, there will be universal submission to His authority and universal admission of His claims. Then will the word of Jehovah in Isa. xlv. 23 be fulfilled—" I have sworn by Myself, the word is gone out of My mouth in righteousness, and shall not return. That unto Me every knee shall bow, every tongue shall swear."* A king does not reveal, save unto his nearest and dearest, his secret purposes concerning his son, and the fact that God is pleased thus to reveal the secret of His purpose is surely a supreme proof of His "Abounding toward us in grace . . having made known unto us the Mystery of His Will according to His good pleasure which He hath purposed in Himself." How great, then must be this purpose !

The next verse tells us when it will be introduced, "in the Dispensation of the Fulness of Times." God has not only His way but His time. He is never too early and never too late. It was in the "*fulness* of time " that He sent forth His Son (Gal. iv. 4). It was in "*due* time " that Christ died for the ungodly (Rom. v. 6). He will come again, as Son of Man, in the day known to the Father (Mark xiii. 32). And so here, God has determined "the Dispensation of the Fulness of Times " when all things shall be headed up in His beloved Son.

* This quotation is specially noteworthy as one of that important group of passages which identify Jehovah of the Old Testament and the Lord Jesus of the New, as the same Divine Person (see also Zech. xii. 1-10 ; Heb. xi. 26).

• Divine Dispensations.

It may be of help to us to here trace very briefly the Dispensations which have preceded this, the last and the eternal one. Dispensations are periods distinguished from one another by the special character of God's dealings with man. God knew from the beginning what was in man, but man must have opportunity to shew what he is. He must also be revealed to himself, otherwise he might complain that he had never been properly tested. The Dispensations have been characterised by a complete breakdown on the part of man, and by mercy and judgment on the part of God. They have been varied and progressive, and in them God has revealed Himself in different ways and degrees.

Conscience.

When man fell, he started on his career of four thousand years' probation, under the power of Satan, who had deceived him; with a corrupt nature within and a blighted creation without; with a knowledge of the eternal power and Godhead of the Creator from His works, and a knowledge of approach to God by sacrifice; with neither law nor government; but with a knowledge of good and evil, fruit of the fall, but unable to avoid the evil or attain the good, apart from the grace of God, but with that grace at His disposal. We may call this the Dispensation of *Conscience*. Men boast to-day that their conscience is sufficient. They were left to its guidance for two thousand years. The silver thread of grace ran throughout, but man's ways were marked with violence and corruption, and the flood at length swept the race away.

Government.

The next Dispensation was that of *Government*, entrusted to man in the person of Noah. But Noah's early failure and the general revolt of mankind under Nimrod, proved Government as powerless to control man as Conscience had been. Judgment fell again at Babel in the confusion of tongues. The era of the nations began with conflicting ambitions and strife, as is witnessed until this day.

Law.

From these nations, a special people was called out, in whom man might be submitted to a new test. Surrounded by every safeguard and many privileges, with Jehovah dwelling in their midst, they received the Law at His hand. Would not man with his conscience thus instructed and his conduct regulated by a holy *Law*, bring forth fruit to God? No, for we are told "they rebelled and vexed His Holy Spirit." Instead of good fruit, "they brought forth wild grapes." Instead of glorifying the Name of Jehovah, they caused that Name to be blasphemed among the Gentiles, and were judged accordingly. The kingdom was taken from them, and given to the Gentile powers.

Christ.

A remnant returned later to their land to be put to a new test—the *Real Presence of the Messiah.* This was man's final test.   The law had said, "Thou shalt love the Lord thy God with all thy heart . . and thy neighbour as thyself."   Christ presented Himself in this double character.   "The Word became flesh, and tabernacled among us."   "He went about doing good and healing all that were oppressed of the devil."   How did men respond to such grace ?   The Cross was the answer.   Man at his best, in the person of the religious Jew, "crucified the Lord of glory."   After that, it is absurd, as well as unscriptural, to talk of man still being on "probation."   The four Dispensations of Conscience, Government, Law, and Christ, have shewn not only that there is something wrong with man, but that there is no good thing in him, and that no good thing can come from him.   What must be done with him then ?   He must either be judged, or treated on terms of purest grace.

Grace.

The descent of the Spirit initiated the Dispensation of *Grace*.   Only in Christ, dead and risen, can any good be found.   Christ is all in all for those who will receive Him.   Most reject Him.   Some respond and become a people to His Name, "the Church of the living God."

Mercy and Judgment.

This Dispensation will end in the coming of Christ for His saints, and the great Apostasy of Christendom, already ripening, will be followed by a short Dispensation of *Mercy and Judgment*, when God's judgments will be in the earth, and He will make them drink the mixed cup of Psa. lxxv. 5. Of this period we have the prophetic outline in Rev. vi.-xviii. Israel, restored to their land, will be blessed materially and spiritually (Joel ii. 19-32), and, through the faithful ones among them, will issue to every nation a worldwide testimony of the coming King. The dispensation will close in the full manifestation of evil in the Man of Sin and Antichrist, who will be destroyed by Christ at His coming in judgment.

The Headship of Christ is viewed in at least five different ways in Scriptures. (1) *Headship in the Hierarchy of Rule.* "Christ is the Head of all principality and power" (Col. ii. 10). This is His present relation to everything that God recognises in the universe as rule and authority. He is the Ruler of rulers. When He comes, He will bear the title, "King of kings and Lord of lords." God has placed Him "far above all principality and power and might and dominion" (Eph. i. 2), including the power of Satan's kingdom, which seems to be an imitation as far as may be of the Divine (see Eph. vi. 12). "Christ is over all, God blessed for ever" (Rom. ix. 5). To Him as Son of Man is this place granted. He could say, in resurrection, "All authority hath been given unto Me in heaven, and on earth" (Matt. xxviii. 18 R.V.). His authority is already recognised in heaven. Even now, He is there called "the Prince of the kings of the earth" (Rev. i. 5), whether they will it or not. All are responsible to Him now, and to Him they will one day give an account of the way they have used their power.

(2) *Headship in "the One Body."*—"Christ is *Head of the Church*" (Eph. v. 23).   There is no union between Christ and the "powers that be," but there is true spiritual union between His members and Himself.   The body began to be fashioned at Pentecost after His death, resurrection, and ascension, and all who have believed in Him since, have become members of that mystical body, united to the Head and to all the other members. The process by which this is brought about is the baptism in the Holy Spirit (1 Cor. xii. 13), and the moment at which this baptism takes place in the history of a saint, is the moment he first believes in Christ.*   The agent is Christ Himself.   "The same is He which baptiseth with the Holy Ghost" (John i. 33).   Writing to the Corinthians the apostle says, "For in one Spirit were we all baptised into one body, whether we be bond or free."   Christ holds the members for their final salvation.   If one member were lacking, the Church might be "holy," but she could not be "without blemish."   She must be both. The members hold the Head for communion and edification (Col. ii. 19).

(3) *Headship in the Hierarchy of Service.*—"Christ is the *Head of the Man*:" that is, of course, not of man in the sense of mankind, but of "the man," the male believer.   "I would have you know," writes the apostle, "that the head of every man is Christ,

---

* It is quite erroneous to cite the twelve disciples of John at Ephesus (Acts xix), in order to prove that Christians may now be in the same state they were in then. They only knew the baptism of John.   They were not "in Christ" at all.   To them Christ was merely " One who should come after " John. No Christian can be in this state to-day. There are no disciples of John now.

and the head of the woman is man, and the head
of Christ is God " (1 Cor. xi. 3). In "the Body,"
Christ is Head of the woman and of the man on
equal ground ; in fact, in this spiritual relation,
" there is neither male nor female " (Gal. iii. 28).
But in social, family, and church relationships, the
difference is recognised and provided for. Here,
there is a hierarchy of authority. Christ as the
Servant is subject to God, so the man to Christ, and
so in her service, whether in the home or in the
church, is the woman to the man. Where this
godly order prevails, how striking is the testimony
of angels and men ! Where it is reversed, how
grave is the loss both here and hereafter ! This
authority is not autocratic, but transmitted. The
man himself is " under authority " to Christ. It is
not a question of capacity or intelligence, but of
godly order. While the woman's strength is in
influence, that of the man is in administration,
therefore the woman is " not to usurp authority " or
" have dominion ("R.V.) over the man (1 Tim. ii. 12).

(4) *Headship in the Place of Responsibility.*—Christ
is the *Head of the House of God.* This is " the spiritual House " of 1 Pet. ii. 5. Christ is the Living
Stone, and the Head Stone of a house formed of
living stones. " The Stone which the builders
disallowed, the same is made the Head of the
corner " (v. 7). No other " house of God " is recognised in the Epistles, as existing to-day. Christ is
a Son " over His (God's) own house " (Heb. iii. 6,
R.V.), and the proof of being living stones is con-
tinuance. " Whose house are we, if we hold fast
the confidence and the rejoicing of the hope firm

unto the end " (Heb. iii. 6). The Lordship of Christ in the House of God is an intensely practical truth, yet too often ignored. "Why call ye Me Lord, Lord," He Himself asks us, "and do not the things which I say?" To acknowledge Him as Lord, is to obey His Word (1 Cor. xiv. 37).

The last aspect of Christ's Headship is, *His Headship of Universal Authority.*—This is the side of truth we are now considering. "We see not *yet* all things put under Him," but all things will be, for it is God's "good pleasure, which He hath purposed in Himself." Christ will yet become the Source of all blessing in a universe of bliss, the Centre of many and varied circles of the elect and redeemed of all ages, the Object of universal contemplation and worship,

Well may this be called "the Mystery of His Will," for such a glorious climax had never "entered into the heart of man." That one born as a Babe in a village stable, and afterward a homeless Stranger in a despised province, "rejected" by His own nation and handed over by them to a foreign power, who killed Him by the cruel and shameful death of crucifixion, should prove to be the long-expected Messiah, the heir to David's throne, the Saviour of the world, and "God manifest in the flesh ; " all this is truly wonderful and utterly incredible to the carnal mind. Yet it was all foretold in the Old Testament Scriptures and confirmed by angels at His birth ; that His kingdom should stretch from sea to sea and from the river to the ends of the earth, that it should last as long as the sun and moon endure (Psa. lxii. 8-17): that not only

Israel, but the Gentiles, should bow beneath His sway, had been sung by the psalmists and prophets of old. But that His kingdom should have height as well as breadth, and be heavenly as well as earthly, should include "all things that are in *heaven* and that are in the earth," and be conterminous with the infinite universe of God, were surely surprising and altogether unlooked for developments, which go far beyond the highest thoughts of the saints of the Old Testament times. This is, however, the purpose of God for Him whom He delighteth to honour, for " He hath put all things under His feet and gave Him to be the Head *over all things* TO the Church which is His body, the fulness of Him that filleth all in all " (Eph. i. 22). "*Head over all things in the Church.*" All these glories He possesses for the advantage of the Church, who shall share with Him the inheritance. This she will enter on in association with Him when He comes. He will come to set up His kingdom, not as the messenger of peace, but to make war, and as the Stone cut without hands to crush the Gentile power; not to sprinkle them with His atoning blood, but to sprinkle His garments with their blood, as He takes vengeance on them. Thus the air will be cleared as after a terrific thunderstorm for the establishment of the Kingdom, in which all will be "headed up" in Christ. What the characteristics of His kingdom are, we shall now consider

There are four things we may notice about the Kingdom of the Lord Jesus Christ, as it is presented in the Word. They are (1) its Progressivity, (2) its Stability, (3) its Eternity, and (4) its Universality.

1. The Kingdom will be *Progressive.*—The millennium—the dispensation of the kingdom glory—will be only a first stage. Then the Lord will reign "in the midst of His enemies" (see Psa. cx. 2). This stage corresponds rather with David's reign than with Solomon's. Satan will be chained, but sin will be present. The powers of death will be limited, but death itself not yet destroyed. Righteousness will first "reign," but later on it will "dwell" among men. As David's reign ended in rebellion and judgment, so will the millennium, for multitudes will only have yielded a "feigned obedience." Before Solomon's reign was finally established, judgment was executed on the Adonijahs, the Joabs, and the Shimeis. It will be only when Satan has been finally dealt with, the wicked dead judged, and all hostile powers, including death and hades, cast into the lake of fire, that the Lord Jesus will deliver up the kingdom to God. And this is not, as has been often taught, in the sense of relinquishing the reins of government, but in the sense of restoring and presenting it to God, purged from every sin and freed from every foe. But "of the increase of His government and peace there shall be *no end* . . to order it and to establish it with judgment and with justice, from henceforth even for ever" (Isaiah ix. 7).

2. The Kingdom will be *Stable.*—Do not the names of Him on whose shoulders the government shall be, assure us of this? "His Name shall be called Wonderful, Counsellor, the Mighty God, the Everlasting Father, the Prince of Peace" (Isa. ix. 6). The stability of the universe will be guaranteed by

the fact that He who holds the sceptre of the universe is "God manifest in the flesh." There are four kinds of equilibrium known to us. The first is what is termed by scientists *labial equilibrium*—that is the condition existing in an infinite fluid, the ether of space. This may be taken as corresponding to the ultimate equilibrium guaranteed to the universe by the fact of the omnipontence of God. Then there is what is called *neutral equilibrium*, that of a ball, which is always in equilibrium, but only by being never really so. This is the condition of the fallen creature—the prey to every impulse—powerless, hopeless. Then there is what is known as *unstable equilibrium*, that of an object balanced from below, like a stick on the hand. Such was the equilibrium of the heavenly and earthly creations under the hegemony of the highest created beings in their particular sphere, Lucifer and Adam. This balance once lost can never right itself. The creature in responsibility, unless in dependence upon God, has always failed, but God has ever had His resource in "the Man of His right hand, the Son of Man whom He made strong for Himself" (Psa. lxxx. 17). This is *stable equilibrium*, that of an object sustained from above, as is a pendulum. However great the free oscillation may be, stability is secured. The stability of the universe will be guaranteed by the pierced Hand that will sustain it from above. And by that same Hand we can be sustained now. Sin can never again appear in the universe of God. And yet God's creatures will not cease to be free moral agents, but they will delight to glorify Him and do His will of their own free choice. Exactly how this will be brought about, may not be absolutely clear. It is certain that all traces of evil nature will be removed from the redeemed. They will be holy as God is holy. They will hate sin, as He hates it. But besides this, I believe there will be two great deterrents ever present to the universe, one an eternal proof that "God is Light"—the awful reality of an eternal hell—perpetual monument of the fearful effects of rebellion against God, of the justice and necessity of which all will be convinced, and the other an eternal proof that "God is Love," the blessed reality of an Exalted Redeemer—the Lamb upon the Throne. "Wherefore we receiving a kingdom which cannot be moved, let us have grace whereby we may serve God acceptably with reverence and godly fear: for *our* God is a consuming fire " (Heb. xii. 29).

The Kingdom of Christ will be *Eternal*. This is an all-important truth, and yet, strangely, it has been overlooked and even denied. It was noticed first, and with perfect reason, that the kingdom prophecies of the Old Testament could not be exhausted in the millennium, with sin and death still present realities. Then the verse already referred to, I Cor. xv. 24, " Then cometh the end, when He shall have delivered up the kingdom to God," was explained as necessarily meaning that after that point, the reign of Christ would cease. To meet the difficulty, a period called the "dispensation of the ages " was imagined and inserted between the end of the millennium and the beginning of the eternal state. But this whole theory, known ˙as

"After the thousand years," is founded on a mistaken premise. "Delivering up the kingdom" does not mean "handing it over," but "presenting it to God." The same word is used in v. 3, "I delivered unto you first of all," where it is evident that the apostle did not relinquish the Gospel, which he presented to others. This act of Christ will take place immediately after the Great White Throne judgment, when He shall have put down all rule and all authority and power—of which the last is death itself (vers. 24 and 26). Then the Lord will present the kingdom back in all its pristine, nay, in enhanced beauty to God. The "till" of verse 25, does not limit His reign to the putting down of His enemies, but guarantees His power finally to put down these enemies. The expression, "the dispensation of the ages of the ages," is quite a fanciful one, as descriptive of any period short of Eternity, for "the ages of the ages" is the Greek idiom for Eternity, and nothing short of it. Words are merely counters. Usage stamps them with their value. It is surely something worse than silly to translate such an idiomatic phrase as "ages of the ages" literally, and yet that is what the "Revisers" have done in their margin, and are thereby, I doubt not, largely responsible for the generally loosened hold of the solemn truth of eternal punishment among professing Christians. In Gal. i. 5; Phil. iv. 20; I Tim. I. 7; 2 Tim. iv. 8, Heb. xiii. 21; Rev. i. 6; v. 13; vii. 12, where honour, glory, and dominion are ascribed to God, we have this subtle marginal gloss—"Greek—to the ages of the ages"—suggesting, though not affirming, that the Greek does not really mean "for ever and for ever." But we may ask, is there a vestage of a hint in any one of these places, that the glory of God is to be limited to a certain period? The same phrase is used of the judgment of the Great Whore (Rev. xix. 3), of the torments of Satan, the Beast and the False Prophet (Rev. xx. 10). And in Rev. i. 18; iv. 9; x. 6; xv. 7, of the existence of God and of Christ, where the same marginal gloss is inserted, "Greek—Unto the ages of the ages." Do the Revisers then suggest that God's existence is not everlasting? Is it not clear that Eternity is stamped on every occurrence of the phrase? To this let us hold fast, for it is the Word of God.

The *Eternal* character of the Kingdom of Christ is further shown in the following Scriptures. The expression is applied in Rev. xi. 15 to the reigning Christ, by the voices from heaven. "The kingdoms of this world are become the kingdom of our Lord, and of His Christ; and He shall reign *for ever*. And to the same truth we will call three other witnesses —(1) King David, speaking of the kingdom of One greater than Solomon, writes, "They shall fear Thee as long as the sun and moon endure *throughout all generations* . . His Name shall endure *for ever*" (Psa. lxxii. 8-17). It is clear that the idea of the reign ending, is specifically rejected. (2) The prophet Daniel is the next witness. "In the days of these things* the God of heaven shall set up a kingdom which shall *never be destroyed*, and the

---

* There cannot be a fifth world empire outside the countries of the old Roman Empire, therefore it is clear that Germany will not and cannot succeed in her ambition to rule the world.

kingdom shall not be left to other people . . and it shall stand *for ever*" (Dan. ii. 44). "His dominion is an *everlasting dominion,* which shall *not pass away,* and His kingdom that which shall *not be destroyed*" (chap. vii. 14). (3) The angel Gabriel confirms this, for he affirmed to the Virgin Mary of her Firstborn, "He shall reign over the house of Jacob *for ever,* and of His kingdom there shall be no end." There can, therefore, be no doubt of the everlasting character of the kingdom of Jesus Christ.

4. The Kingdom will be *Universal.*—It will include "all things things that are in heaven and that are in earth"—that is the whole moral universe of God. When it is a question of submission, "things *under* the earth" are added, for the infernal powers, the lost of angels and of men will be included, but such will be for ever excluded from the kingdom. Those who teach that some Christians will be excluded too, on account of a lack of faithfulness, really shut them out from salvation for ever, for the kingdom is only another term for the heavenly state. All believers will by grace enter into that kingdom "which God hath prepared for them that love Him," but their *place* in that Kingdom will vary with the dispensation in which each has lived and with their individual faithfulness. But Christ in all things will have the pre-eminence. He will be crowned with many diadems, and without one discordant note, the whole universe of bliss will proclaim His worthiness and His praise. And this will continue for ever.

"And every creature which is in heaven and in

earth, and under the earth,* and such as are in the sea, heard I saying, Blessing and honour and glory and power be unto Him that sitteth upon the throne, and unto the Lamb for ever and ever. And the four living creatures said Amen! And the four and twenty elders fell down and worshipped Him that liveth for ever and ever."

"Now unto Him that is able to do exceeding abundantly above all that we ask or think, according to the power that worketh in us: Unto Him be glory in the Church by Christ Jesus, throughout all ages, world without end. Amen."

* Quite a distinct expression, from that already referred to in Phil. ii. 10.